Long Stays in
FRANCE

Long Stays in
FRANCE

A COMPLETE, PRACTICAL GUIDE TO
LIVING AND WORKING IN FRANCE

DOROTHY PHILLPOTTS
AND ROSALIND MAZZAWI

HIPPOCRENE
BOOKS, INC.

DAVID & CHARLES
Newton Abbot   London

HIPPOCRENE BOOKS
New York

British Library Cataloguing in Publication Data

Phillpotts, Dorothy
  Long stays in France.
  1. France
  I. Title II. Mazzawi, Rosalind
  944.083'8

  ISBN 0–7153–8993–9

Printed in Great Britain by
Billings and Sons Ltd Worcester
for David & Charles Publishers plc
Brunel House Newton Abbot Devon

Published in the United States of America
by Hippocrene Books Inc
171 Madison Avenue, New York, NY 10016
ISBN 0-87052-596-4

Contents

Editor's Foreword

While we have been considering up-to-the minute trends, and studying the document '1992 Aujourdhui' issued by the French Ministère Délégué Chargeé des Affaires Européennes, with its generous plans for a Europe without frontiers, the British Government has been dragging its feet so much that no-one on either side of the Channel can now guess what the eventual role of the British will be in the Europe of tomorrow. But although this is painful politically, practically it seems to have had a positive effect, with more people being genuinely interested in living in France than ever before, so that *Agents immobiliers* in the north have actually begun to paste the words 'Estate Agents' on their windows, and are issuing sale particulars in both French and English, as if 1992 had already arrived.

Of course, in a book of this length we cannot hope to cover completely the brilliant panorama of life in France, but we attempt to get into focus many under-appreciated regions, linking these briefly with an outline of the scenery, weather, food and drink, and investigating the possibility of jobs and housing in the country as a whole. Although at the present time the advice we give about commercial prospects cannot be very precise, what we have to say about advance research is rather important – when my husband and I first became *propriétaires* in the Dordogne twenty-five years ago, in a France we thought we knew, it was more leisured, more conservative and much more limited than the dynamic France of today. Here, for many years, although we had good French friends, we were content to remain foreigners. This old-fashioned France, a world of many interlocking élites, which we can trace in films, literature and the arts, tends to be the one that people dream about after a few holidays devoted to wine, food and culture, but it is less and less the France of today.

A quiet but effective industrial and cultural revolution has been going on for some years now, where art and ideas exist alongside the search for a new identity sometimes so strong that it can break down the old insensitivity between class and class, or between the people of the north and the people of the south. To a certain extent, if you once settle down in this new France, you will not feel foreign, and you can make your own way.

It is a pity that we cannot go deeply into the question of French nationality and citizenship here, for there are many things to be weighed up. However, this question does at least remind us that once a house has been bought in France, at one's death it will be as if one had always been French, for the estate will be administered by French Law and not according to any will that has been made in your country of origin. Since hardship can result from this, we give some particulars about the law of inheritance in our Appendix on househunting.

I have been most grateful for assistance from a wide circle of friends in France and England, and the most helpful topographical and geographical works of reference are listed in the Bibliography at the end of the book.

I should like particularly to thank the French Government Tourist Office, especially Patrick Goyet the *Représentant General*, Pauline Hallam and her colleagues, for considerable help given over the many months I have been collecting material – not forgetting the indispensable assistance that has also been offered on the spot by *Syndicats D'Initiatives* all over France. There, too, I received most useful up-to-date advice from Keith Wilson, English estate agent in Le Bugue, as well as from Paul and Jenny Dyer, and a real fund of wisdom, both national and local, from M. Philippe Gunet and his family. The French Embassy in London most generously supplied essential information about French plans for 1992 in connection with the *Marche intérieur*.

In conclusion, I must warmly thank my co-author for her text 'Life Day by Day', as well as the Traditional Crafts Guild for struggling to produce the Rivers and Regions Map, and Valentine da Costa for her patient work on a difficult manuscript.

Dorothy Phillpotts

Part I
MAKING PLANS

Dorothy Phillpotts

Rivers and Regions of France. (*Traditional Crafts Guild of Cardiff*)

1
Why Go To France?

When the European Single Market gets into its stride, the trickle of people looking for a life on the other side of the Channel may well turn into a flood, and since citizens of any member state get preferential treatment, this transfer from one country to another has become remarkably easy. But opinion polls about living in France tend to show up all sorts of errors of judgement – plans that might have been better avoided, an odd preoccupation with inessentials, or facts that simply have been wrongly combined – all things that could be checked in advance.

The main trends are what one might expect. Most UK residents who are seriously planning a long stay in France think first about the weather. 'Sunshine' is the popular demand, and then, as an afterthought, 'a mild winter'. But only half of those who make this reply realise that whereas sunny and even scorching weather can be relied on in much of France throughout the summer, that exact combination is more or less restricted to the coasts of the far south and south west. The implications of this are discussed in chapter 2.

At this point, too, perhaps it should be noted that only a knowledgeable minority appreciates fully the wide choice of terrain available. Not only are the truly magnificent landscapes the most diverse and exciting in Europe, but they are extremely thinly populated, with only 49 persons to each square kilometre. Comparing this with the population of England – some 361 person per square kilometre (Wales has 135 and Scotland as few as 65) enables one to grasp more easily the elusive atmosphere of relaxation permeating all the country districts. This atmosphere must have changed little over the centuries, and is particularly marked in formerly remote provinces that have been opened up by the good road systems of today.

With an area that makes France the largest country in Europe – 212,300 sq miles (550,000 sq km) – every taste can be satisfied: deep gorges, great forests, mighty dunes, rushing rivers, extinct

11

volcanoes, and alpine national parks with wonderful flora and fauna – all have their attractions. And in the backwoods of less spectacular regions are innumerable smaller but perfect satisfactions – vineyards ripening at the edge of golden maple trees, prehistoric dolmens on heather brightened moors, or perhaps an ancient stone dovecote just visible in a thick chestnut wood – things such as these make up a richness of gentle scenery that evokes a word all too rarely heard in Britain – *tranquillité*.

Such *tranquillité* is no longer the preserve of those who live in hamlets, or are leisured holidaymakers. With the present decentralisation of industry, more and more jobs have become available in the *Centres Commerciales* of quite small towns adjacent to splendid stretches of countryside, transformed for modern living, perhaps not for the better scenically, but certainly for the betterment of local people. In such towns the municipalities have organised social centres, large sports fields, swimming pools and even *sports nautiques* upon the local rivers, most of which would be envied by residents in parallel British towns. Even the smallest towns now have supermarkets that genuinely cut the cost of basic foods and commodities. Larger towns and small cities, reorganised since the sixties in much the same style but on a larger scale, have hypermarkets selling everything from bedroom furniture to mouse traps. Here, too, you will find the multi-national firms which may from 1992 be extending the job market.

It would be a mistake to suppose that this modern France is a totally new France, concerning itself only with the evolution of a technocracy. The graph of technical advance has gone up and down since the eighteenth century, and to-day's 'industrial revolution' merely completes yesterday's trends that were too often frustrated by the sheer weight of the agricultural community. Less than a century ago, 50 per cent of the French nation were peasants. By 1949 this figure had dropped to 33 per cent. Today only a million and a half farms remain and the people who run them like to think of themselves as *propriétors*, and not mere *fermiers*, which gives them both prestige and security, if not exactly economic equality with their brothers in industry.

So the 'new' industrial workers are actually only one generation away from the farm, but have inherited a life their parents never guessed at. Television helps to form their tastes and extend their outlook. And their patriotism, which is acquired early in life and cemented by the central system of education, is blossoming in an extraordinary way as they reach out for the France that was once the sole preserve of the aristocracy and *haute bourgeoisie*. This France, with its deep roots in intelligence and artistic performance, could grow stronger and stronger as more people begin to participate in wider values, and the 'liberty, fraternity and equality', which long enshrined the privileges of only half the nation.

Food comes next on the list of popular questions we're all at home with, for though the average foreigner is almost bound to overlook the typical French atmosphere until he has visited France a number of times, he has usually thought a lot about gastronomy, whether he dreams specifically of the best French cuisine, or quite simply of good food and drink with a daily bottle of inexpensiye wine to round off his idea of a good life. And here something extraordinary shows up. We are accustomed to think that the cost of living is higher on the other side of the Channel (which to us just means a big food bill), but in fact prices in the UK and France are becoming closer. At the top end of the market (in England that means 'eating out'), our prices are vastly more expensive, and rising all the time.

In France, where the standard of restaurant cooking is exceptionally high, one can have a most delicious meal for something like a third of the price charged at equivalent establishments in southern England. (Scottish and Welsh restaurants do not yet charge south country prices – and rarely provide French quality food!). Young expatriates with well-paid jobs soon realise that the saving in restaurant bills will more than make up for any extra cost of food eaten in the home and, given the low cost of wine, for a small extra outlay they can live at an altogether higher standard than is achieved in Britain. But budgeting is such a highly individual matter that it might be a mistake for those on lower salaries to think along the same lines, despite the fact that what you lose on the roundabouts you tend to gain on the swings, and the necessary 'free circulation of goods and services' which we all look forward to under the Single Market guaranteed by the European Community *L'Acte Unique* of 1987 will certainly affect us all, in one way or another.

However, those who plan to retire to France and can make detailed advance research, at least need have no fears about spiralling house prices, although the Single Market is almost bound to affect this too in time. More and more house agents in London are handling French properties, and more and more French *Agents Immobilier* speak English and, while prices remain as low as they are at the moment, now is the time to consolidate vague plans.

Half of the houses in France have been built since 1945, mostly in the new suburbs of old towns and cities. Though much of the style of development has been deplored by those in architectural circles, who think that a great opportunity has been missed, one must respect the effort and understand that, in order to grow from a major agricultural country to a top industrial power, many long cherished ambitions have had to be sacrificed. In some places it may have looked as though the sacrifices were in vain, but now, forty five years after the war, the wheel has turned full circle. France has the right to feel satisfied with her progress, and the direction in which she has gone. The housing available reflects a remarkable historical period, and what you go for now may be full of surprises. It is still possible to find small and large nineteenth century town houses that have not been gutted too indiscriminately in order to incorporate questionable improvements, but perhaps the thing to hope for most is an uninhabited old farmhouse that has remained in the family as an undeveloped *résidence secondaire*. There are many permutations on these two themes for those not tied to one special region. And a stroll around the streets of some small provincial town can produce surprising bonuses. Neat, double-fronted houses with shining knockers and tidy gardens present an impeccable, antique face, and the question, again and again, of who could possibly live in them? One suspects retired generals, doctors and more lawyers than the town could possibly support, and is aware once again of how little one knows about the French themselves.

As an amateur anthropologist I have long puzzled on the real differences between the French and the English, trying to find a key to open both locks; eventually I found myself on common ground, but it is difficult to describe. There are so many wrong ways of thinking about the French that perhaps it is helpful to mention a few that can be changed practically. Anxious newcomers should never be put off by blank stares and lack of smiles. Have you ever considered what a strain the average French-speaking foreigner puts upon his listeners? And just how difficult is it to understand your own particular version of French? As perfectionists, the French long to know what you are actually talking about, and to get it right, and the stare and the frown are quite understandable. If at the outset you could arm yourselves with a few sentences learned by heart, explaining your difficulties with the language, and asking for help, you would be surprised at the help, encouragement, and even friendship that could be offered.

Other people whose grip on the language is perhaps better than average have been known to complain that they can't get a word in edgeways, and that the dotting of every i and the crossing of all the ts must spring from too great a sense of superiority. Here one is really up against it, for what is at fault is the language itself. All those subtle sounds and complex nuances need facial contortions quite foreign to the English speaker. The French are imposed on by their own language to such a degree that they appear to stick out their lips belligerently when all they are trying to do is make a perfect vowel sound. If they can be justly accused of liking the sound of their own voices too much, it is only true to the extent that well spoken French is almost hypnotic in character. It carries one away. Watching French television will make all this more familiar. Of course, it cannot be emphasized too often that we'll never understand another person without a common language, and would-be expatriates can't start too early to brush up such rudiments of the tongue as they have already acquired. A more or less painless way of making progress is to listen regularly to the French radio programme 'France Culture', and at the same time extend your vocabulary steadily – such an effort is possible even for those who are never likely to master all the grammar.

It has been said that too many people wishing to live in France see it in terms of history and what they learned about at school, and not as the country that actually exists today. One author, at least, can throw light on this. He is Theodore Zeldin, Fellow of St. Anthony's College, Oxford, and famous for his two-volume *France* as well as for *The French* published in 1983 (for all his foreign sounding name, he is British). This funny, deep, shocking and profound book should be read by everyone interested in living in France. One finishes it with regret and an urge to investigate for oneself. Zeldin points out that the French have become sensitive about their lack of popularity with many of their visitors, and his

15

generous impartiality is welcomed with an awareness that our own national characteristics are no easier to live with, and with thankfulness for the new spirit abroad in this rather difficult field.

We cannot hope to do justice here to the treasures of France, the art, architecture and artefacts, the châteaux, gardens and churches. They are better cared for than they were a decade or two ago, and in the little country museums and galleries there is a new expertise and pride. The great regional museums, looked after by local government, have never been better.

Understanding the French becomes easier if we know how the regions are governed. There is no doubt that the centrally organised education, and three tier administration of the country, reflects a sort of systemization that has deep roots in the French character (but if you were a present-day psychologist maybe you would put this the other way round).

France was divided into twenty-two main regions in the 1960s to provide a modern cohesive framework for the economic development of neighbouring *départements*, and to assist in the effective decentralisation of industry. Since that time some of these regions have been further linked to provide even greater efficiency – Rhône-Alpes is probably the best example – where one very large area can cater for every conceivable aspect of modern life and financial expansion.

The *départements* – and there are now ninety-five – originated just after the Revolution, when in order to wipe out the memory of the old feudal overlords, and to destroy even the flavour of the *ancien régime*, with its excessive, unfair taxation, it was thought desirable to give entirely fresh names to the new centres of administration. The re-welding of these *départements* into 'regions' has happily brought back several historic provincial titles, Languedoc, Provence, and so on. In fact these had never disappeared culturally, but their official re-emergence, and their use by tourist bodies, has tended to strengthen local feeling and give a welcome fillip to inter-*départemental* co-operation.

Writers often attribute the original invention of the *départements* to Napoleon, but the statesman and political genius Mirabeau was responsible actually for their inclusion in the Constitution of 1791. (It is interesting to recall that he admired the British form of constitutional government and even studied it in England.) The *départements* were given a regional flavour by naming them after local rivers, mountains and coasts. Domestic administration of *départements* today is still maintained by an advisory committee known as the *Conseil Général* (a body that dates back to the time of Napoleon); this is elected every six years but is directly responsible to a *préfet* (another Napoleonic title) who has considerable power. This *préfet* is appointed by the government, and is assisted by a staff of civil servants.

Between each *département* and the man in the street is the municipality or *commune*, a basic unit of local administration. Every *commune* (and there are some thirty-eight thousand of these) elects its own municipal council (again serving for six years) and its *maire*. The *maire* is the principal administrator of the *commune*, supervising public works, police and so on, and in this he is immediately subordinate to the *préfet*. In the larger communes, the powers of the *maire* and local council are limited by professional civil servants; the budget, in any case, is approved by the *préfet*. It is interesting to visit the *préfecture* in a *départemental* capital city to see how the three-tier system works and to get a glimpse of the French civil service at its best. But it is no less interesting to find yourself in the tiniest rural *mairie*. (There are something like two million civil servants altogether, though nearly a million of these are teachers.)

Everyone who has recently motored around France will have encountered large placards with polite messages about public works from the *Conseil Général* to the inhabitants of its *département*. These supply a colourful inkling of what has been developing since the sixties – but more particularly since the Socialist coalition rose to power. The regions have had more money to spend on road surfaces right across the country, an expenditure appreciated by everyone.

At the hub of power in the Republic is the President. Elected for a period of seven years, he appoints both the Prime Minister and the Cabinet, and he has powers to dissolve Parliament. As head of State he enjoys unique and supreme privileges, and during his term of office M Mitterand has authorised some imaginative projects which truly reflect his power and his vision. Posterity will probably hail the pyramid extension to the Louvre as the most popular, but the new National Library, still in its early stages,

17

may well become the most enduring monument to the dynamic end of an epoch.

The French government is responsible to a National Assembly (the Parliament), which consists of a Chamber of Deputies, elected by the people for five years, and a Senate, or Upper House. Senators are elected every three years by general councillors and delegates from the municipal councils.

Politically inclined expatriates may decide after a while to apply for French citizenship and thereby make a contribution at the end of this three-tier chain of administration, but this is a big step, needing much consideration. Perhaps the most important pre-condition is that you should have lived in France for at least five years.

Meanwhile, it is important to get to know the country as a whole before understanding where one can best fit in. In the next chapter, a purely geographical tour is taken as the basis for research, since the study of watertight *départements* and larger economic regions tends to introduce artificialities. Tourist literature can be helpful as long as it is realised that it is thoroughly subjective, concerned primarily with a bird's eye view of marketable assets.

A few hints about regional food and wine, and a list of *départements* are given at the end of each section.

2
Living In a New Landscape

A surprising number of people happily search for jobs and university careers in foreign countries without knowing anything about the year-round climate, density of population and local susceptibilities.

All too often, geography, topography, recent history, and what one might call day-to-day human possibilities are set aside because of financial prospects, and the final choice may owe rather too much to the subjective recommendations of acquaintances and a dream of the future based on wishful thinking.

So what will you look for in a country so large and diverse as France? And if dream jobs could materialise in an ideal landscape, have you thought out in detail where your preferences lie?

Clearly some kind of lightning tour is necessary for aspiring foreigners who are still more or less ignorant about the pros and cons of different regions. Perhaps we should start by examining the weather, before looking at the scenery, beginning with the cities and coasts that became hosts to our own great grandparents more than a century ago.

Climate

Acquiring accurate information about Continental weather is more difficult than it might be, partly because local tourist organisations can only offer weather charts that give monthly averages for both temperature and rainfall, linking these to the more famous cities and resorts, while quite reasonably ignoring the land mass and the influence of the winds. Since the lowest day-to-day temperatures for quite large areas are rarely published (and even if they were, would be rather difficult to obtain), most of the people settling in France have only the sketchiest ideas of what to expect out of season.

Among the more common mistakes is an assumption that very hot summers will necessarily be linked to mild winters, or that scorching weather will gradually give way to a long, temperate autumn, so that phenomena such as snow and biting northerly winds, arriving without warning on an autumn day in valleys adjacent to alpine foothills, can be a most unwelcome surprise. This may not matter to holidaymakers or businessmen, but what if a new resident has to get young children off to school without a car? Similar inconvenient instances, arising solely from ignorance of the weather, can be multiplied.

Fortunately, not every surprise is unwelcome. Consider places like South Brittany, which is fairly far north, but definitely influenced by the warm waters of the North Atlantic Drift, bringing equable weather in autumn and early winter.

In fact, France has a particularly wide range of climate owing to its situation between the Atlantic Ocean and the Mediterranean Sea, its relation to the rest of the Continent and the variety and height of its mountains. The weather down the west coast is known as western oceanic, having moderate rainfall, less frequent in summer, and relatively equable temperatures. The temperate climate of north-western France, which we feel we understand, is nevertheless affected by the size of the land mass, so that in high summer the weather appears to be consistently hotter than in the UK, more or less verging on the extremes of continental climate as one travels further and further east. Here there is a brilliantly coloured autumn in the Ardennes and the Vosges before the advent of a freezing winter, particularly in Lorraine, which is the price that Central Europe has to pay for its baking summers. Going south and west through Franche-Comté, along the borders of Switzerland, there is snow all the way for five months of the year, melting into a late and wet spring, and more baking summer months in the unjustly neglected Jura.

The Mediterranean climate of the Côte d'Azur is typified by hot, dry summers and mild, wet winters. But although geography books state that the north or north-westerly mistral funnels down the Rhône Valley, it actually brings rain to the coast of the French Riviera further east, reaching as far as Nice, although most of the winter rain here comes from Italy – 'le vent d'Italie'. In autumn and spring this rain is quite heavy. The mistral itself is particularly tiresome west of Toulon, where it is icy and eccentric, blowing itself out in three, six or nine days (a hundred years ago it once blew for fourteen months without a break). Not for nothing was it called 'the master wind' (from the Latin *magister*). It is known to have stopped trains, and once propelled an engineless train from Arles to Port Louis, as well as blowing down bridges and carrying away flocks of sheep. Expatriates thinking seriously of retirement to the Riviera should consider avoiding both the Rhône and the western Côte d'Azur if they suffer from the kind of rheumatoid arthritis that is sensitive to north winds. Snow falls in the higher mountains of Provence in midwinter, something that is completely impossible to imagine in midsummer.

Although the Côte Vermeille beyond the Rhône lies at the foot of the Pyrénées, the coastal weather here is surprisingly unaffected by their proximity, though it has its own wind, the tramontane, which only seems to be known locally. It is fairly harmless, blowing briskly for several days, but after heavy storms can bring enough rain to flood coastal campsites, and empty them overnight. In winter it is also extremely cold.

There are several special pockets of weather along the Pyrénéan range which do not fit in with formal explanations about mountain climate. Noteworthy is the peculiar clarity of the air and continual bright sunshine at Font Romeu in the Cerdagne (a kind of high plateau between 4,000 and 5,250ft [1,200 to 1,600m] above sea level). This has made possible remarkable experiments connected with solar energy. At Odeillo is an enormous parabolic reflector composed of 9,500 mirrors trained on a target some 60ft (18m) away. In winter, Frot Romeu is a popular ski spot.

No less remarkable is the freak weather of Biarritz on the border of the Basque country near the Atlantic end of the Pyrénées, which is more influenced by the oceanic climate than that of the mountains. High daily temperatures, year round, and almost constant sunshine, make up this enviable micro-climate. Some rain falls in February, March and April, but not enough to spoil Biarritz's reputation as a winter resort. Figures in London's *Financial Times* during the last few years show winter temperatures for November and December and January similar to spring temperatures in London, February being the coldest month of the year, with an average of 9.4°C (49°F) – similar to the beginning of May in London – or June in St Moritz. Average monthly temperatures have in some years been higher than in Nice and Palermo, both famed for year-round heat.

First time visitors to these delectable places are often surprised to see so much snow on the heights in August. Col de Tourmalet,

21

which is the highest road pass, closes from December until June, and because of its tortuous road and dangerous bends, large vehicles are discouraged at all times. Even some of the lower passes are shut until June, and Col d'Aubisque actually closes very early in the winter, in November.

But adjusting to life in high altitudes needs far more than a common-sense attitude to snow. Low clouds can be very dense in the autumn and spring, and even in midsummer, causing accidents to humans, stock and motors.

'Continental' weather starts a few miles north of the Pyrénéan foothills and embraces all of the coastal area. Very high temperatures may alternate with exceptionally heavy storms and rain at the end of summer. This is particularly true in the Dordogne, where a stifling July may herald a soaking August, though in some recent years drought, the dreaded *sécheresse*, has held into late autumn. The sudden cold may arrive in October or may hold off until November, but severe weather is not experienced generally until after Christmas. Once again, snow in high places is not unusual and is common over a wide area in the Massif Central, often holding until after Easter. Easter in the Dordogne can have flurries of snow, too, but the weather there is just as likely to be *riant* – smiling – ushering in an unexpectedly sunny and warm period, with a dry north wind.

Snowfields in the high Alps of Savoie and Dauphiné need no introduction, and, once again, the classic description of mountain weather – 'cool summers and cold, sunny winters' – does not really apply. Summer is generally fine and hot, with temperatures rising very high on cloudless days, resembling a characteristic continental climate. Lakes have a water temperature of above 22°C (72°F). Snow falls heavily on the lower mountains but is lighter on the higher slopes around Mont Blanc, but as the whole region is efficiently organised for the winter sports industry, there is very little disruption of traffic.

Specialised knowledge that can profit the interested amateur concerns night-time cooling of the slopes, causing katabatic winds (down-valley air currents). Up-valley winds – anabatic – can trigger off thunder storms. In some places characteristic mountain breezes are a dependable feature of the local weather. The height of the snowline is determined by a combination of katabatic winds, precipitation, temperature, humidity and sunshine. The French understand all of this very well, and have exploited fully what they claim as the largest organised ski area in the world. This comes pretty near to harnessing the climate in the service of man.

Southern Perspectives
Provence - Côte D'Azur
It's just about a hundred years since the coast of Provence, which once had been an outpost of ancient Rome – 'Provincia Romana', was given a new name, 'La Côte D'Azur,' though this then referred to the entire seaboard from Genoa in Italy to Marseille, and not to the shorter stretch between Menton and Cannes which we all know to-day. Since that time, the picturesque small fishing villages have disappeared, and the decorative bays with their pink rocks and brilliant blue seas have sported innumerable pleasant villas, intermingled with wooded peninsulas hiding more spacious residences in sub-tropical gardens, as well as newer resorts with high density housing. Only during the last twenty years has some of the wooded and mountainous hinterland of this coast begun to fill up with smaller houses a little too close together, some built as *résidences secondaires* (which now seem to have become a must for many better paid workers) and some as 'first time' retirement homes.

Twenty-five years ago my husband and I researched this coast at the unfashionable end between Bandol and Cassis (which actually is still a fishing port) but we were too late for the sort of 'undeveloped' house we had hoped to find, although inland we passed many old pantiled cottages with vine covered arbours in the ancient Provençal style. One headland was being cleared of succulent vegetation, and stakes with numbers already indicated a fairly large housing lot. In fact the French have done this sort of development rather well, often in the shape of an old-style fishing village with plenty of split levels and cunningly concealed courtyards. By now there will be houses of this kind available for purchase over a very large stretch of coast, but scarcely ever at a 'bargain' price.

But what of the great towns and cities further east, the 'real' French Riviera? Menton, a favourite town of mine, lies in a bay which the Romans called the 'Gulf of Peace' and is so built that a mountain view is to be had at the end of many a principal street – in fact the mountains come down almost to the edge of the city and constantly invite one to go off and explore the villages of the lower heights. Here rich lemon groves give way to olive trees, pinewoods and scrub oak. There is a charming legend which tells how Eve, having picked a lemon when she was expelled from Paradise, hid it until she came to this well-wooded and well-watered place, and soon all the slopes and valleys were covered with scented lemon trees. The Mentonnais will tell you that semi-tropical fruit will grow here as nowhere else in Europe, and in February, at Carnival time, a Lemon Festival is held. Good museums, music festivals, excellent exhibitions, and an interesting old town, all contribute to the relaxed atmosphere very suitable for the retired, but necessitating an above average income for anyone who would like to settle down here permanently.

Those who do not want large towns, however interesting, could profitably explore further inland. Old houses can still be bought in the high Parc National du Mercantour, which has a boundary with Italy. Further to the south east, in the Massif de L'Esterel, and the Massif des Maures, the remains of fine pine forests still exist. Though destroyed by summer fires from time to time, they are frequently replanted. Between these two massifs, the hinterland of Fréjus and St Aygulf has attracted speculative builders, and overdevelopment is on the way.

And those tempted by the big names – sophisticated Antibes, Cannes, St Tropez, and so on – mustn't forget that the huge volume of tourist traffic during the summer season, with its attendant crowds and parking problems, makes these otherwise brilliant spots pretty unsuitable for year-round residence. On the other hand, Nice, with its long Italian history, fifth largest town in France, and capital of the Riviera, has so much to offer permanent inhabitants who want an urban background. A mild winter, good airport, fast trains, every possible kind of sport, club and museum, plus three libraries, and a special service for the retired – 'Troisieme Age' – with care associations linked by telephone (93. 16. 12. 05) make this historic city especially suitable for those who do not have to economise.

The Alpes of Hautes Provence contain one of the wonders of France – the 13 mile (21km) long Grand Canyon of Verdon – 10 mile (16km) south west of Castellane. In some places the cliffs drop 2,300ft (700m) – roads have been built along both sides, and the wild splendour of the scene is difficult to describe.

Castellane would make a good shopping centre for enterprising spirits settling in some isolated house on the somewhat desiccated terrain. Three roads run at varying levels along the steep coast between Nice and Roquebrune. The Middle Corniche has the finest views, and it is this road that serves Eze, one of the mediaeval 'perched' villages. Only five years ago, several of the ancient houses were *A Vendre*, and at that time fifty or so people overwintered there, but now it has become a 'fashionable' place to visit. Other perched villages, even more remote, can suffer from being almost completely empty throughout the winter when they actually may be snowbound, and this is a question on which you should satisfy yourself completely before making any kind of offer for a property. Residents all along the Riviera warn their friends to negotiate only with long-established agents (see chapter 5 *Setting Up House.*)

Marseille, second city of France, but more of a typical Mediterranean port than anything else, full of local colour, with yachts in its Vieux Port, and plenty to stare at, is nowadays uncomfortable and overcrowded, with two communities consisting of recent immigrants and old inhabitants, who can barely speak to each other, and crime continually erupting. There are therefore political problems at the *maire* level. Some say that Arabic is almost as much its language as Provençal. Today's rich cosmopolitan mixture includes Armenians and old bourgeois merchant families, plus the recent immigrants – *pieds noirs* – from North Africa. Excellent museums include the Musée D'Archéologie for the Mediterranean as well as the Musée of Old Marseille. One of Le Corbusier's rare buildings, Unité d'Habitation, is on the Boulevard Michelet, which is near the Parc Amable Chanot in the south of the city.

Food: bouillabaisse and bourride (fish stews with garlic) are the regional dishes par excellence. Olive oil from the local trees, sweet peppers, herbs and garlic dominate the cuisine; and Pissaladière combines these ingredients in a tart with anchovies. Glacé fruits and marzipan calissons. Brousse de la Vésubie and Tomme Arlesienne Cheese from Aix.
Wines: favourite Côtes de Provence wine is the château bottled Rosé; Cassis produces the best white and Bandol a full-bodied red. There is also plenty of cheap, everyday Vin du Pays and some sparkling whites from the Côteaux d'Aix-en-Provence.

Départements: Alpes de Haute Provence, Hautes Alpes, Alpes
Maritimes, Var, Vaucluse.
Principal towns and cities: Aix-en-Provence, Cannes, Marseille,
Menton, Nice, Toulon.

Up the Rhône
The Ile of Camargue between the Great Rhône and the little
Rhône, at the delta of the river, is rarely given its full name.
It is composed mostly of marsh and lagoon and continually re-
news itself from the sands and mud brought down by the River
Rhône, which, after meeting the Saône near Lyon, runs swiftly,
at something like twelve miles an hour (19kmph), all the way to
the Mediterranean.

Here are bred the small white horses with particularly large
hooves suitable for the wet terrain, as well as the black bulls used
in the *courses libres*, a dangerous 'game' between boys and bulls
played out in the Arena at Arles. Both horses and bulls roam wild
in the marsh and their *gardiens* are wide-hatted cowboys in the
Wild West tradition.

The big, low farms, or *mas*, have long been associated with
stock rearing, but since France lost Indo-China, the cultivation of
rice has become important. Despite the fact that the mosquitoes
that breed here have been 'treated', and reduced in number, they
are so ferocious that few people will willingly live on the marsh if
they have not been bred to it.

From afar, Aigues Mortes, one of the few settlements on the
delta, looks like a *château*, but it is a genuine town completely
enclosed by fortress walls that were built by Philip the Bold on
the site bought by his father, King Louis, in 1241, and used as
an exit port for the Crusades. It is now 3½ miles (6km) from
the sea, to which it is connected by canals. Salins-du-Midi has
a depôt near here, and the great peaks of salt are very much in
keeping with the bizarre overtones of the area. On the other side of
the marsh, behind Saintes-Maries-de-la-Mer, a pilgrimage centre
for the gypsies of all Europe, is the Parc Ornithologique on the
Etang de Vaccarés, famed for its flamingoes. Arles, at the head
of the Delta, was once the capital of Roman Provence. Tourists
flock to see the enormous arena, Roman burial ground and other
remains, and art lovers make pilgrimages to the museum and
special exhibitions in memory of Van Gogh.

Northbound travellers take in Nîmes and Avignon naturally, the former almost swamped by developments on the periphery, which although they barely show on current 1:200,000 maps, slow the heavy traffic circulation to a frustrating crawl. But the splendid Roman city has endured despite many vicissitudes, including the Wars of Religion, which actually ruined the medieval town. Fortunately the planning of the public gardens in the eighteenth century rescued the Spring of Nemausius and the Roman baths, and gave the great arena and the perfect Maison Carrée breathing space, but modern Nîmes, alas, is no longer beautiful and always seems in a hurry. Is it an accident that *'denim'* – de Nîmes – was invented here?

By contrast, everything in walled Avignon seems peaceful, though this can be deceptive because the town is near enough to Marseille to be affected by its criminals. Every year large bands of tourists flock to see the Palace of the Popes, the cathedral, museums, and so on, and the exclusive-looking shops add to a vivacious, atmospheric city. Exploring on the plain in the vicinity reveals many restored cottages and houses treasured as *résidences secondaires*, while due east about 31 miles (50km) away is the Lubéron Regional Park, an attractive mixture of market gardens, fruit trees, forests, perched villages and steep-sided valleys.

Travelling north along the west bank of the river opens up many escapes into the high Ardèche, a mixed countryside from south to north, and just below Roman Orange (which in fact lies to the east in a landscape of oak trees and olives) is that famous wine, Châteauneuf du Pape, from a vineyard shadowed by the ruined Keep of the Popes' summer residence. Further to the east rises Mont Ventoux.

From Pont St Esprit a road runs along the little-known Gorges de L'Ardèche with high balconies of terraced vines and many desirable cottages here and there. The bridge, half a mile in length, was built as the result of a shepherd boy's vision, and was famous throughout all medieval Christendom.

Exploring beyond Bollène will bring you into the Baronnies, above Ventoux, and around Nyons, with its extraordinary and original church, you will find a riot of flowers and market gardens in a corner of Provence little penetrated by foreigners. Eroded slopes, lavender cultivation and perched villages all have their place as you return westwards into the Tricastin, known as the gateway to Mediterranean France, where the handsome *château* of Grignan adds a welcome note of sophistication. Here lived and died (in 1696) Madame de Sevigné, writing her life away in the letters to her daughter that were to make her famous. Desolate houses for redevelopment can still be found in this area.

Further north still there is a very steep road beyond Aubenas and Vals, so dramatic and dangerous-seeming, as it climbs out of the deep valley, with enormous drops to the south. Both towns, but especially Aubenas, with its view and traditions, could be tried as a base in various seasons. In fact there are many small towns and villages where foreigners have chosen to live in the last few years but after the baking summers the hard winters have sometimes been met with astonishment and despair.

Historic Valence on the Rhône's east bank, with its Romanesque cathedral and Renaissance houses, a market centre for the fruit and vegetables you see all along the river, is now a centre for light industry. The steep hills which rise on opposite sides of the river lead into corniches of the Cévennes, twisting and turning among arid slopes and chestnut groves which connect finally with pastoral scenery around Gerbier de Jonc, a strangely shaped mountain 5,090ft (1,551m) high, at the source of the Loire.

Now the importance of the vineyards of the Côtes du Rhône begins to make itself felt more and more (see under *Wines*, below). Lyon, in its bowl of hills, the second largest city of France (population 1,200,000), lies between these vineyards and those of the Beaujolais. There has been great expansion here during the past twenty-five years; some southerners look upon it as the capital of France. In keeping with its expanding industries, high technology, important universities and medical school, the approach from the west is through developing suburbs, not very pretty, but the centre is still fine, with its two dozen bridges (mostly rebuilt after war destruction) spanning the rivers Saône and Rhône, where they meet to form a peninsula. Here the tree-shaded quays are lined with the sixteenth and seventeenth century mansions of the great silk merchants. One of these houses, the Musée des Tissus, displays woven stuffs from Byzantine times to the present day. Today, of course, prosperity also depends on the synthetic materials that mean more jobs, and many of the mulberry trees that once fed silkworms have now been replaced by vines.

But the aura of its silken past has never completely left Lyon, and the peninsula is packed with exciting architectural mementos of its brilliant history, from Place Bellecour, one of the largest squares in France, to the splendid Musée des Beaux-Arts with its exceptional collection. On the west, Old Lyon mounts up the steep Fourvière hill, and beyond the peninsula on the opposite side the busy commercial centre skirts the ugly suburbs of high rise flats – Villeurbanne – though today's workers can leave town by a galaxy of motorways to restored town or country houses in the quiet Monts du Lyonnais and Bas Dauphiné.

Food: from start to finish this is a major gastronomic area. Vegetables baked in olive oil as ratatouille or tian, and many dishes *'à la provençale'* with tomatoes, garlic, olive oil, onions, aubergines and herbs go hand in hand with the culinary marvels of Lyon, where there a particularly high number of restaurants with stars. Poulet from the Bresse, poularde demi devil (chicken with supreme sauce). Cheese from Mont d'Or.

Wines: from Côtes du Rhône include the white Condrieu and Château Grillet; red Hermitage and Crozes-Hermitage, but the choice is too wide to list here. Beaujolais from the north of Lyon is becoming a favourite but is not always genuine.

Départements: Ardèche, Bouches du Rhône, Drôme, Gard, Rhône, Vaucluse.

Principal towns and cities: Arles, Avignon, Lyon, Nîmes, Orange, Valence, Vienne.

Across the Pyrénées and Languedoc

The historical province of Languedoc disappeared during the Revolution. It reached its highest peak long ago, in the twelfth century, when, before it was defeated by the barbarians, it stood for *parage* - 'food for all, kindness and sweetness of life'. It was a vast territory, bounded by Clermont Ferrand in the north. Its successor, the economic region Languedoc-Roussillon, more or less hugs the coast, though in the north it also takes in the Lozère with its remote, arid *causses* and picturesque canyons of the rivers Tarn and Jonte, which have only been fully accessible during this century.

The name 'Languedoc' referred to the Provençal language of the region, which at one time was spoken as far as the Loire – 'oc' of the south meaning 'yes', instead of the 'oui' of the north. It still survives as the 'patois' of rural districts, but since it has diminished a regional movement has arisen seeking recognition of the cultural distinctiveness of the south of France and the 'Occitan' language. 'Occitanie' is said to cover one third of the national territory, with three fairly distinct local dialects, but it is mostly middle-aged people who use these, although 21 per cent of all the French like to think that they speak their regional language well. Actually, when the unification of France was achieved in the nineteenth century, a quarter of the inhabitants spoke no French whatsoever. In fact, the French accent in Languedoc (described as the 'accang') is very harsh and is difficult for even competent French speakers to understand at first.

Upon arriving in this ancient region from Provence, it seems especially suitable first to visit Montpellier, a most pleasant city and cultural centre, called by some 'the Oxford of France'. With a university dating back to the thirteenth century, an outstanding medical school, the oldest botanical garden in the country and an annual opera season, as well as fine town houses (mansions known as hôtels) and the famous Musée Fabre (the best picture gallery in the south), it is an especially agreeable retreat for the intellectually inclined.

Behind the coast of Languedoc is what you might call the wine plain. There are vines as far as the eye can see. It has often been said that there are no important wines between Provence and the Pyrénées, but here the generous Corbières have been much improved in the past decade. Mile after mile of rough hillside, with many a village and little town, and interesting Narbonne, once a great port and now 12 miles (19km) from the Mediterranean. Carcassonne, the enormous, restored medieval fortress, has become an important city with some 42,000 inhabitants.

France first built her great new resorts on the coast of Languedoc-Roussillon, starting with La Grande-Motte near Montpellier, and then Port Barcarés and Port Leucate in the sixties and seventies, utilising the salty lagoons and marshes that had cut off the ordinary traveller from long sandy shores. Now, as at Cap d'Agde, with ambitious pyramidal architecture, very well done of its kind, and bristling with yachts and every sort of distraction, they're a kind of rival to the Côte D'Azur, but for a more budget-conscious market. Some lagoons are still preserved for migratory bird populations. Fortunately the development was government-supervised and started with the extermination of mosquitoes.

Nearer the Pyrénées, in the valleys of the Tet and Tech, vast market gardens have taken over from the vineyards, producing early peaches, cherries and pears, and beyond Amèlie les Bains, a spa in the Upper Vallespir, chestnut and beech woods give way to a panorama of endless peaks in Spain.

Here you are in Catalan France – it was part of Spain until 1659. In summertime at the village fêtes you may run into a dance called the Sardana, from Catalonia, but you will discover it quite certainly and rather more ceremoniously at weekends in the handsome Loge de la Mer, a kind of town house in Perpignan. Some pleasant old buildings from Catalan times have survived here. The local French dialect is mainly Catalan and can be difficult to understand. Actually the Spanish inheritance here was strengthened by the many refugees who settled during the Spanish Civil War. There is now recognition for Catalans as a separate ethnic group with a bilingual culture of their own, something they share with the independent Principality of Andorra, further to the west in the Pyrénéan mountain range, which is governed by representatives from France and Spain known as the 'Co-Princes'. Today these are the Bishop of Urgel (which lies just over the border at the edge of the Spanish Pyrénées) and the President of France.

Locally, Andorra is known as 'the valleys', much of the region being inaccessible and surrounded by high peaks. Until after the last war, when the mountains began to be exploited for winter sports, it was entirely cut off from France throughout the winter and snow covered the central passes of most of the Pyrénées sometimes from November until June. Today the central valleys are being somewhat over-exploited for tourism, with flats for summer visitors and the recently developed winter sports centres lining the highway.

The Pyrénéan range has been described as a mountain cushion which grows higher and wider from west to east, ending in a drop of nearly 10,000ft (over 3,000m) within view of the Mediterranean, and regularly divided by valleys perpendicular to the main crest line. The reality, from one's feet or car, seems vastly different. Vast summits rear up, such as the Balaitou – 10,322ft (3,146m), Vignemale – 10,820ft (3,298m), Posets – 11,062ft

(3,372m), Maladetta – 11,168ft (3,404m) at the Aneto peak, the highest point of the range, and several more. On a clear day, arriving from the north, the range can be seen from far off, impressive in its width and height across the landscape. Close at hand the peaks disappear, but one regains them on climbing up the valley.

The majesty of some high valleys is without equal in other parts of France. Snow persists until June, and on the peaks it remains year round. Near the Col de Tourmalet, which could only be crossed by sedan chair until the end of the eighteenth century, the Spanish irises push through as the snow melts. Because of the profile of the land, with no connections between the perpendicular valleys, cultivation follows its ancient pattern with self-contained communities utilising pastures in the mountains and sharing the agricultural land in the valleys. The coming of hydro-electric schemes has prevented a complete drift from the land. Tourism has brought some wealth as well, especially in the hinterland of Lourdes, though so far it is in a lower key than in mountains elsewhere.

Spas also, which fifty years ago were in decline, are being rejuvenated. Some of these in the foothills have an almost Mediterranean climate with palm trees, bougainvilleas, etc. These spas cater for a wide spectrum of diseases that are often resistant to medical aid – respiratory ailments, skin diseases, rheumatism, as well as many others – and they are beginning to enjoy a revival.

Perhaps the long Pyrénéan winter has too much against it when it comes to considering some of the pretty little towns as ideal spots for retirement homes, but the great beauty of the national park in the centre of the range, well to the south of Lourdes, would tempt both walkers and naturalists. (Lourdes attracts some of the three million pilgrims annually seeking a miracle cure from the grotto of Ste Bernadette.) It is always crowded around the famous Cirque de Gavarnie in high summer and local travel can be uncomfortable. Luz St Sauveur, with pleasant local walks, has various new developments. Most of the ideal barns and old farms, etc, have already been developed as *résidences secondaires*.

However, some of the larger towns make capital out of their mild winter weather. Pau has beckoned the English over a long period. It has a panoramic view of the Pyrénées and is famous as a year-round health resort. As capital of the Pyrénées Atlantiques *département*, it has grown in importance since the discovery of natural gas at Lacq. An English church and an English library have survived until now.

Biarritz, on the Atlantic Coast (once the favoured resort of princes), has a favourable micro-climate with remarkably temperate winter weather (see also *Climate*, p19). It has every luxury, casinos, golf courses, museums and the deeply interesting Basque country on its doorstep. No-one knows where the Basques and their unique language originated. On their feast days they are perhaps exhibiting the long vanished customs of the twelfth century with their dancing, songs and poetry.

Food: in the west, goose fat is predominant in local cooking and foie gras (goose liver) dishes are specialities. In the east, olive oil takes over, and throughout the region garlic and spices are common. Chorizo is a very spicy sausage. Jambon de Bayonne a delicacy. Collioure Sauce is mayonnaise flavoured with anchovies. Pepper, tomatoes and herbs and many vegetables follow the Provençal trends. Roquefort cheese.

Drink: Armagnac - older than the brandy from Cognac (the best labels are from *Bas*-Armagnac, not Haut Armagnac – quality develops with age). Jurançon wines (south west of Pau), Blanquette of Limoux (a sparkling wine older than Champagne). Sweet wines of Roussillon, VDQS wines of Minervois, white, red or rosé.

Départements: Languedoc Roussillon: Aude, Gard, Lozère, Hérault, Pyrénées Orientales. Midi Pyrénées: Ariège, Gers, Haute Garonne, Haute Pyrénées, Pyrénées Atlantiques.

Principal towns and cities: Biarritz, Carcassonne, Foix, Lourdes, Montpellier, Narbonne, Pau, Perpignan, Tarbes.

Southern River Country
It is the central part of the southern river country that seems to charm the average foreigner more than the whole of the rest of France put together. It was the Dutch who first dug themselves in to the Dordogne when they toured south after the Second World War, but the English quickly followed suit, pleased with the specially friendly welcome of the local people and delighting in the ever-changing scenery. This fascinating landscape encompasses winding streams and pastures at the foot of low hills, small stone townships, and then the higher limestone *causses*, bare plateaux

which have never borne much more than juniper and box-trees, and which overlook wide beckoning distances where countless hamlets, three or four hundred years old, are lost to view. Empty stone houses can still be found in the area.

Here the River Dordogne is the main stream of a river system that rises in the Monts Dore, at the foot of Sancy, highest peak in the Massif Central, and after crossing the high Limousin plateau finds its way through gorges, forests, fields and vineyards until finally it reaches the great Gironde estuary near Bordeaux on the west coast. Travellers meeting the unremarkable landscape at the western end would not guess at the combined delights that await them further east, though the vineyards that cover almost the entire Gironde *département* have a charm all of their own, and the first sight of hilly St Emilion, wreathed in vines as far as the eye can see, arouses the right kind of anticipation for what is on the other side of Bergerac.

But Bergerac, lying comfortably in the wide alluvial plain, is important in its own right. As centre of the large local tobacco industry, it has the only experimental tobacco institute in France, as well as the only tobacco museum, and is the main commercial and shopping centre of an extensive area.

Eastwards, now, the land begins to be less flat. Visitors who delight in maps will seek out the special marvel of the *Tremolat* cingle, or giant loop, in the Dordogne river, which can be best seen from a wooded bluff above the village that reveals a checkered countryside of intensive cultivation, market crops and tobacco, and the wide river itself, host to water ski enthusiasts and many other river sports. Beyond this meander, the central stretch of river begins to show its paces – here is a reach with scalloped limestone cliffs falling sheer into the waters and there an ancient village with a castle, possibly dating back to the tenth century, possibly only to the nineteenth century, a combination that will be repeated again and again upstream.

Near Sarlat, in its narrow glen, you are in ancient Périgord Noir, the name describing woods of evergreen Holm oak, many long since cleared. The name, perhaps, also denotes the cultivation of the black truffle, delight of gourmets, for this is a region where eating ranks very high indeed, and here you must sample the restaurants along with the little medieval streets.

But west and north of Sarlat, in a large angle enclosed by

the rivers Vézère and Dordogne, is the most important area of the whole river country – Les Eyzies, which has been called both the 'University' and the 'Capital' of pre-history – and Montignac, whose cave of Lascaux (discovered as recently as 1940) is the most important painted cave in the world. After descending by steps to a great depth you reach four chambers containing remarkably lively paintings that have taken advantage of curved rock surfaces to add relief to the bodies of bulls, deer, cows, bison and ibex. It is believed that these date back to the Magdalanian and Aurignacian cultures of the Paleolithic Period – the Chipped Stone Age of 40,000 years ago.

For thousands of years these paintings must have remained at a constant temperature, for their preservation was perfect, and it was not until tourists arrived in large numbers that deterioration set in. Then, in 1963, to prevent exposure to artificial lighting, to humidity, and the introduction of carbon dioxide (from human breath) the caves were permanently closed. Now an exact replica of Lascaux has been constructed so that the ordinary visitor to the area can still appreciate this extraordinary achievement of our distant ancestors. Other caves at Les Eyzies, with fewer paintings, operate a system of restricted admissions.

But probably the medieval period, with its great castles and pretty manor houses is the main attraction for the expatriate. Beynac, on its dizzy height above the river, was once an English base for supporters of Richard Lionheart. Later, the great bully Simon de Montfort (father of the English historical personage of the same name) dismantled it, and when the actual river banks marked the battlelines between the French and English in the Hundred Years' War, the latter were ensconced in Castlenaud Château.

You will meet Richard Lionheart again on the central reach of the River Lot, which runs in a series of loops roughly parallel to the River Dordogne, 31 miles (50km) to the south. The country is rather remote and often more majestic than the Dordogne Valley, with deeper forests, and wild, savage plateaux, alternating in the far east with alpine-type pastures. Many of its villages have attracted new inhabitants from the north of France, but fewer English, although an increasing number bought houses in 1988 and 1989.

The Romans named this region *Acquitania*, the land of waters, for the cliffs that lie beneath the limestone plateaux are pierced by what are known as resurgences, innumerable springs, cold as cold. At Cahors the Chartreuse fountain is still carried under the river to give drinking water to the town. This spring, in the days of Gaul, was worshipped as a goddess, and the importance of water is commemorated everywhere by the naming of countless towns and villages with a name ending in 'ac'. The active history of Cahors dates back to the Middle Ages, and its towered Valentré bridge is a most remarkable medieval survival, although the construction you see dates primarily from its nineteenth century restoration. But picturesque small towns and villages, like marvellous Saint-Cirq-Lapopie on its dizzy height above the river, stem from the fifteenth century, or even earlier, and their little towers, dovecotes and archways, all miraculously substantial, draw you back.

Dropping south from the Lot brings you to the real country of the Midi, vast orchards, sunbaked, where the farms watered by the Garonne have a Roman appearance, with great shallow roofs of ancient pantiles. Montauban, pleasantly situated on the Tarn, further east, is another centre for fruit marketing. It also has an important museum – the painter Ingres was born here. Albi, also on the Tarn, has made a place for itself in the artistic and industrial world. Toulouse Lautrec's works (he was born *here*) are housed in the episcopal palace next to the extraordinary fortress cathedral that hosts a *Son et Lumière* performance every summer. Most of the gorges of the Aveyron to the north west (even less known than the Lot) have no roads, but can be viewed across the tops of trees and plateaux. Cross the landscape here via the interesting city of Rodez, capital of Aveyron *département*, with its pedestrianised streets behind the pink cathedral containing a nest of jewellers' shops, boutiques and good food, and so to the gorges, or canyons, of the River Tarn, the finest of them all. Further on, near the source in the Lozère mountains, the country is wild and bare, baking in summer, freezing in winter, but nearby are the great chestnut forests of the Cévènnes.

From the south, the gateway to this entire area is Toulouse. Built around a bend in the River Garonne, it is encircled by the Midi Canal. Fourth largest metropolis of France, it was the capital of old Languedoc and has an ancient university which is the second largest in France. It is famous for its aerospace industry. Despite the rise of industrial apartments on the new approach

roads, the lively heart of this rose-pink pantiled city has not fallen
to developers, and its courtyards, fountains, shaded squares and
architectural masterpieces provide an age-old background to the
lively concerns of today.

Food: In Périgord Noir, the canning industries at Périgeux and
Sarlat preserve truffles, foie gras, poultry, mushrooms and fruit,
the best of which are still available locally at farms and markets.
Walnuts and walnut oil are an important production. Lard is used
in much of the cooking.

High gastronomy attracts gourmets from all over France to a
cuisine based largely on the use of truffles, foie gras and superb
vegetables – sauce périgourdine is Madeira with truffles. Many
different kinds of fungi including Cèpes à la périgourdine.

Wine: Cahors wine has a long tradition. Côtes-de-Fronton, Haute
Garonne, are white, red and rosé. St Emilion wines are esteemed
enough to be included with Bordeaux. Bergerac red wines are for
drinking young, and the best white Montbazillac can rival a good
Sauterne, but also should be drunk young.

Départements: Aveyron, Corrèze, Dordogne, Gironde, Lot, Lot et
Garonne, Lozère, Tarn et Garonne, Tarn.

Principal towns and cities: Agen, Albi, Bergerac, Brive, Cahors,
Figeac, Montauban, Périgeux, Rodez.

Down the Atlantic Coast

On this run to the south from Nantes there are something like
400 miles (nearly 650km) of coastline to explore, and a very wide
diversity of scenery encompassing a rich mixture of French life
and history. If you're lucky with weather on your first-ever exploration, you'll get that peculiarly brilliant sunshine which has
given the coast the name of 'Côte Lumineuse'. It has the lowest
rainfall of all the Atlantic seaboard and clocks up a very high
total of summer days every year. Fields of maize and sunflowers
enhance the southern atmosphere. Until relatively recently, few
British travellers came this way, though the French flock in for
their holidays on the extremely varied coast. Maritime industry
is interspersed with sandy shores; oysters, mussels, lobster and
prawns are more or less 'farmed' in shallow beds and there is
the canning of fish. Little places like Marennes, 'the capital of
oysters', just inshore from the Isle of Oléron, have pretty, small

houses in varied styles under a particularly luminous sky, and, provided prospective buyers are not concerned about the smell of fish, there must be bargains to pick up in many places.

If you want to investigate living by the sea, leave Nantes by the D751 and keep going until you reach an attractive old town, Pornic, with some shade from umbrella pine. It's worth returning via St Philbert-de-Grand-Lieu, on a large lake where the marsh reaches as far as the eye can see. This is an echo of that more important stretch of marsh you will meet further to the south, the Marais Poitevin, running west of Niort. When the English ruled Aquitaine, Niort, on the Sèvre Niontaise River, was the port of Poitou, but Atlantic winds silted the river mouth, and without an outlet to the sea, seasonal rains flooded the land. Draining started in the Middle Ages and finished in the seventeenth century, resulting in a checkerboard of canals enclosing very fertile land, intensively cultivated, but with a wet central core. Today, tourism exploits the canals. The Marais Poitevin is a regional park with the grassland used mainly for cattle raising, and there is an important nature reserve.

Poitiers, capital of the region, on the great limestone plain of Poiton, north east of Niort, is an antique Roman city and was already old when Clovis drove out the Visigoths in AD 507. Full of excellent houses and a baptistery believed to be the oldest building in France, it was English for thirteen years under the Black Prince, until 1369. It is particularly famous for its Romanesque churches and the Angevin Cathedral of St Pierre (the style we call Early English), and has been saved by the pedestrianisation of a large area of its centre. Now it has been thrust into the modern world by being on the motorway from Paris to Bordeaux, as well as by Futurescope, a centre of advanced technology with a research institute funded privately by industry, and leisure aspects such as a special cinema for nature films designed in the shape of a crystal, and so on.

La Rochelle has been called the most beautiful port in France; its entrance is framed by large stone towers from the Middle Ages and its quay is lined with yachts. People shop in comfort under the *porches*, or covered arcades, and a good fish market seems to be always open. From here small boats go to the offshore islands, but the Isle de Ré is now linked to the mainland. The larger Ile d'Oléron has a bridge, and *écologistes* rightly declare that this has ruined it. In high season the island is abominably crowded, not only with summer residents but also with day trippers and campers, who crowd not only onto sites but also into gardens and the corners of vineyards. By the mild climate, mimosa and tamarisk bushes, etc, turn Oléron into a true haven in the spring and summer.

The 'luminous' coast finishes with Royan, sheltered by forests on the estuary of the Gironde, a resort that has a brilliance scarcely equalled by anywhere else in Europe. Virtually destroyed during the war, it was magnificently redesigned by leading architects. Splendid beaches are the background for every possible kind of *distraction*, and the sea promenade has good shops.

A few miles away is the most remarkably sited church in the whole of France, on the very edge of a cliff, at Talmont, in the River Gironde. Inland, Roman Saintes is an interesting centre, and neighbour to Cognac, where you will find all the best brandies in France. The surrounding countryside contains a remarkable number of twelfth century churches, many with outstanding carvings.

Across the Gironde estuary is the dead-end peninsula where vineyards produce some of the best Médoc, and in Bordeaux, of course, the greatest wine shippers in the world are on the Quai de Chartrons. This is a handsome quarter, with the cranes and ship funnels at one end and the great splendour of the Grand Theatre, luxurious shops and classical bourgeois mansions behind, in the heart of the city. Eastwards for many miles lie more vineyards and to the west and south, vast sand dunes flank the sea – the highest in Europe. Lagoons and swamps back these dunes, and behind these again are the Landes, 2½ million acres (1,0125 hectares) of artificially planted forest, which came into existence at the end of the eighteenth century when vast sand hills had to be stopped from encroaching on the adjoining land. This 'desert' was anchored with the assistance of hurdles, and the planting of trees and grasses, broom and gorse. There are a few small resorts along the coast and a large one on its own basin, at Arcachon, famous for its oysters. Coastal currents are dangerous, and the Atlantic breakers formidable. Nor are the long straight tree-lined roads conducive to new settlements, although the inland lakes attract yachtsmen and water sports at holiday times, and the one-storey Landes houses are bright with flowers and noisy with geese. The introduction of cork oaks and evergreen oaks has made the pine forests far less monotonous.

For some years there has been an interministerial commission for the development of the Aquitaine coast that actually aims to keep the undeveloped area as a lung where all kinds of appropriate forms of recreation can be expanded, and where there are already facilities for many kinds of sports. In the far south, on the edge of the Basque country, surfing is popular.

Food: dominated by the vineyards of Bordeaux, the lure of good claret has developed a gastronomic centre, with cooking similar to that along the Dordogne; 'à la bordelaise' denotes a red wine sauce with different garnishes. Entrecôte Maître de chai is grilled over vine twigs. Charente Maritime has exceptional seafood. Marennes oysters; Mouclade: mussels in a creamy wine sauce.

Wine: Top claret appellations are pricing themselves out of the market with new vintages at around £24 a bottle. 'Second' wines of the cru classés (top châteaux) such as Margaux and Pauillac can be much cheaper for laying down. Crus bourgeois wines at reasonable prices reflect the greater wines. St Emilion should not be overlooked (see also *Southern River Country*).

Départements: Charente Maritime, Gironde, Landes, Loire Atlantique, Pyrénées Atlantiques, Vendée.

Principal towns and cities: Bayonne, Biarritz, Bordeaux, La Rochelle, Nantes, Rochefort, Saintes.

Across the Centre
The Alps and Franche Comté

The spectacular scenery of the Alps embraces a vast area to the east of the Rhône – great mountain peaks where the snows never melt, alpine pastures, rocky defiles and gentle plateaux. The Southern Alps have a dry Mediterranean climate and, before the advent of winter sports, were very poor; their highest massif is Parpaillon in the Alpes of Hautes-Provence. The Northern Alps are spread over the *départements* of Savoie, Haute-Savoie and Isère. Most of Savoie only became French in 1860, having previously belonged to the Italian kingdom of Savoia. Isère corresponds more or less with the former principality of Dauphiné, which provided income for the Dauphins – a title given to the eldest sons of the French kings since the eleventh century. The lower slopes are intensively farmed and are covered in arable fields, orchards and vineyards.

The coming of electric power changed the economy dramatically, although the valleys were losing their younger inhabitants considerably before the expansion of winter sporting. Since the recent inception of the larger economic area 'Rhône-Alpes', widespread investment in improved sporting facilities on 290 sq miles (750 sq km) of alpine slopes has brought an additional wave of prosperity.

There cannot be a more inspiring way to discover the Alps than to take the northbound road through the Alpes Maritimes from Nice to Grasse, centre of the French perfume industry, first passing through the palm trees, cork oaks and olive trees on the lower slopes, and then past roses on all sides, and fields of neatly spaced lavender bushes scenting the air. In Grasse itself, even the gutters smell sweet, enticing the stranger to visit the factories on a guided tour. All the way there are glimpses of new housing developments.

Napoleon came this way when he returned from Elba in March, 1815, and what must have been a mere track then is now a well-surfaced highway, though very tortuous in parts. Mounting to the Pas de la Faye (3,218ft/981m) awards panoramic views of the Riviera and Provence, and down to Castellane, before the hairpin bends deliver you to Digne, 'capital of the Lavender Alps', terraced Sisteron, the Valley of the River Durance and relaxed Gap. Col Bayard gives a first view of distant snow-capped peaks.

Now there's a choice; if you continue with Napoleon you reach Grenoble, and the autoroute for Chambéry, with its great sweep round into Savoy (*Savoie*) and access to Mont Blanc, at 15,983ft (4,870m) the highest peak in Europe. Grenoble is one of France's truly great cities, with three universities, its own *Grandes Ecoles*, numerous opportunities for technical studies, boundless enterprise, and many industrial successes (electro metallurgy, chemical engineering, etc) stemming from its pioneer work on hydro-electric power in the nineteenth century. Two thousand people are employed at the centre of nuclear studies. The population has multiplied five times in forty years and is partly housed in the skyscraper blocks that stand on wide avenues along which traffic flows effortlessly – but the historic old town on the Isère is still the centre, preserving its Renaissance Palais de Justice and cathedral dating back to the tenth century, and a museum of painting and sculpture of the first rank.

The alternative route north, following the River Durance via the recently-constructed reservoir-lake of Serre Ponçon, brings you to the splendidly situated old town of Embrun, which has all sorts of covetable town houses as well as some new developments. Then, veering north, you reach Briançon, the highest town in Europe. There are new quarters with plenty of character outside the original citadel which guards the pass into Italy.

A second choice from Gap, across a remarkable landscape of alpine pastures and arid peaks, takes you south east to the most recently established of the national parks – Mercantour. The combination of Mediterranean and alpine weather has produced a phenomenal flora, with many plants found nowhere else in France. The resort of St Martin Vesubie, with some fine old houses dating back to the fourteenth and fifteenth century, is skirted by many new housing estates. In the side valleys leading towards Italy are interesting developments in the shape of large Swiss-style wooden chalets. Winter sporting is popular here, but is in its infancy.

One of the loveliest, largest, and least known of all the national parks – Ecrins (for lovers of real solitude) – lies in a triangle formed by Briançon, Bourg l'Oisans and Gap. The highest peak, Barre des Ecrins, is 13,463ft (4,102m).

The spectacular route north, via Italy's Mont Cenis, brings more and more peaks into view. On the edge of the area enclosed by the Vanoise Park (between Moutiers, Bourg St Maurice and Val D'Isère) are innumerable new 'villages' of apartment blocks built specifically for winter sports, and the area attracts all kinds of developments – offshoots of the tourist scene, clothes and equipment – as well as budding hoteliers.

Accessible from Peisey-Nancroix, a genuine village with old wooden chalets, the park is also favoured for summer walking, and below the village is a famous and welcome viewpoint for the mighty snow-coverd Mont Blanc massif. Keen skiers opting for early retirement should research in the Chamonix district further north for ski runs available year round.

The fauna of all the parks hereabouts include chamois, ibex and marmot, and the golden eagle and ptarmigan etc. The last bear was killed in Vanoise in 1921. Wolves and lynx were common a hundred years ago, and the latter are being re-introduced, to the dismay of shepherds. Among the flora, the rarer plants are the lady's slipper orchid and martogan lily and the rarely seen *Saxifraga florulenta* (mercantour).

From the point of view of permanent residence, it is necessary to understand that though the sun may shine on the mountain tops in the late afternoon of a summer's day, in the shady valleys it can be very cold. Snow may arrive (plus rain) quite early in October and remain on the passes until June. Nevertheless towns like Evian and Aix-les-Bains attract year-round visitors to their thermal springs.

To the south west of Grenoble is the subalpine area of Vercors, where the average altitude is some 3,940ft (1,200m) and Le Grand Veymont peak reaches 7,683ft (2,341m). Erosion has caused unusual and bizarre formations. Low-grade pastureland, sometimes planted with lavender, and vines, and with woods of spruce and beech, lead up to vast and astonishing monoliths. Now a regional park, the Vercors is being developed for tourism and is attracting newcomers for the purchase of *résidences secondaires*. Villard-de-Lans is a pleasant ski resort on a wide plateau. This wild region was a stronghold for the French Resistance in World War II, and the long memories of some inhabitants can be uncomfortable.

Franche Comté is unjustly neglected by most foreigners, largely due to its geographical situation, as the relative positions of Lac Léman and Lac de Neuchâtel turn it into something of a dead end. The mountains of Jura are virtually a plateau some 5,900ft (1,800m) high from which impressive views of the Savoy Alps can be enjoyed, although the massif is actually rather awkward to cross. Gashed by erosion, this plateau is slashed across by defiles known as *cluses* and there is much rocky scenery decorated with waterfalls, and many lakes amid alpine pastures full of flowers in both spring and autumn. The variation in scenery between pale green fields and dark fir trees beneath rocky pinnacles adds up to an unusual sombre splendour.

Besançon was the capital of the old province and is unusually situated in a *cingle* of the River Doubs with hills all round and mountains to the north. Artificial silk was first perfected here in 1884 and is still produced today. Dôle, another attractive town on the Doubs, contains a most interesting museum, birthplace of Louis Pasteur. Houses from all periods since the fifteenth century crowd up the narrow and twisting streets. Many of these towns in Doubs have rather a Swiss air. Gustave Courbet was born on the River Loue at Ornans and his birthplace shows some of his rather dark pictures. Wild boar is hunted near here in the extensive woods. The little autonomous *territoire* of Belfort, right on the German frontier, is now a humming industrial centre, but dairy farming and the timber industry survive.

Food: Dauphinois or Savoyard Gratins, cheese fondue, and queues d'écrevisses (crayfish tails) are typical alpine dishes, in a cream and milk orientated cuisine. Many unusual salmon species come from Lake Annecy and Lac Léman (Lake of Geneva), and quenelles de brochet Nantua (a poached mousse of pike) is a speciality of the Jura.

There are some two dozen cheeses – the popular Gruyère and Emmental, Reblochon and Tomme de Savoie being outstanding.

Wines: include Clairette de Die, a sparkling wine from the south of Drôme, and both sparkling and still wines in the Vin de Savoie appellation, particularly AC Seyssel. Côtes du Jura include red, white and rosé.

Départements – Alps: Alpes de Haute Provence, Alpes Maritimes, Drôme, Isère, Haute-Savoie, Savoie.

Principal towns and cities: Aix-les-Bains, Annecy, Briançon, Chambéry, Digne, Evian, Gap, Grenoble.

Franche Comté: Belfort, Besançon.

Limousin and Auvergne

These sister highland regions running across the Massif Central are somewhat alike in their pleasant lack of commercialisation, their rural economy and their relaxed (though growing) tourism. But Limousin, the lower of the two, is richer than Auvergne, and her wide pastures have long been noted for horse breeding (the Anglo-Arab horse originated in the famous stud at Pompadour). On entering Limousin from the Dordogne, it would be difficult to know where it actually begins were it not for a sudden change in the houses. All at once the steep pitched and mansard roofs have gone, to be replaced by Midi-type pantiled chalets, though in more sober colours than those in the south.

A lot of clearing has been done on the low hills in recent years to make room for fruit growing under EEC grants. Apple trees replace the vines; there is maize instead of tobacco, and the walnut trees are no more. But the chestnut woods are still plentiful and there are occasional plantations of the great red oak. One senses, rather than sees, that one has gone higher. Far to the east there is a glimpse of beechwoods and the Plateau of Millevaches. The landscape rolls, farmhouses are bigger, tall, three-storeyed buildings. Before reaching Limoges one crosses the swift running Vienne, and there are more and more little ponds which have appeared only in the last few years to supply home fishing for the pot. Larger étangs are regarded as beauty spots, and provide every kind of water sport.

Limoges has been growing steadily during the last decade, and housing developments now spread over a wide area – mini towns and villages tacked onto older communes. The intensive industrial growth of the city started quite soon after the war when almost overnight the renowned porcelain industry converted to the use of natural gas kilns and started a new age of expansion; and the uranium deposits discovered in the Ambazac hills resulted in the foundation of Europe's largest uranium-processing plant, at Bessines.

The art of enamelling, and the fine champlevé work first made Limoges a large town in the Middle Ages, and the craftsmen still make individual works of art. In fact it is possible to attend beginners' courses in enamelling and ceramic ware, as well as all the more usual crafts (pottery, weaving, etc); particulars from the Chambre de Métiers De la Haute Vienne, 12 av. Garibaldi, 87000 Limoges, Tel: (55) 77 13 85; as well as from the Comité Regional du Tourisme du Limousin, Tel: (55) 77 58 21, Ext 452. Accommodation is arranged in hostels, farmhouses or even under canvas.

Tapestry work is the other great craft of Limousin, dating back to 1665, when Aubusson was given the title 'of Royal Manufactory'. The famous 'Lady with the Unicorn' tapestries were made here. Local factories may be visited. Courses in the craft are arranged through the Chambre de Métiers de la Creuse, 5 rue de Londres, 23000 Gueret, Tel (55) 52 05 30.

The Volcans D'Auvergne regional park is 75 miles (120km) from north to south and presents an extraordinary landscape of extinct cones in a number of places, one of the most astonishing being near the source of the Loire at Gerbier de Jonc, where the view to the north on a clear day displays tier after tier of volcanic peaks extremely distant. Here you may discover what is a rarity in France – thatched cottages – though the common Auvergne farmhouse has slate or old stone tiles over the rather sombre local stone. During the years after the war, the retreat from the land in Auvergne was so critical that recently special subsidised regional studies became necessary in order, among other things, to lighten the problems of the remaining inhabitants. Every aspect of rural life was reviewed. The smallest communes were helped to build *Salles des Fêtes* and sports arenas. Old people's homes were transformed, and the unpopular HLMs (low price, high rise *Habitations à Loyer Modéré*) built in the outskirts of Clermont Ferrand were rehabilitated. Clermont, the lively capital, headquarters of the vast Michelin rubber company, is expanding round its ancient centre. In a country where so many grandparents still live with their children's families, the solitary aged were not forgotten, and the use of the word 'humanisation' for works connected with the creation of clubs, plus the provision of sitting rooms and restaurants, demonstrates the conscientious advance visible on every side. Efforts to modernise agriculture have gone hand-in-hand with the decentralisation of industries, a new look at training schemes and education, and the provision of new jobs in expanding tourism. Taken altogether, these efforts, though far from complete, have produced a buoyant mood. Many spas are being modernised; winter sports centres are increasing in number. At Super Besse, on the wide plateau near Puy de Sancy, not far from the source of the Dordogne, is a great deal of winter sports development. This particular corner of the Auvergne, which is very near the capital, has everything. St Nectaire, the great twelfth century church with its barrel roof, lies a little to the north. The beautiful Basilica of Orçival is near the spa of Royat and Puy de Dôme, highest of the peaks (4,808ft/1,465m), with a toll road to the summit, all with windswept views of approximately one hundred extinct craters. In the far south, below Puy Mary, the green mountains of Cantal are wonderfully unspoiled, with winter sports well contained at Le Lioran, but with *ski de fond* (cross country) available everywhere between beechwoods and luxuriant mixed forests. Vic-sur-Cère, another spa, has a micro climate boasting unusually dry and sunny weather.

In the least known corner, the gorges of the Allier and the Loire lead travellers up and down, through villages with indescribable views, past Romanesque churches and across an extraordinary railway that miraculously still runs.

Then, when you think you have discovered almost everything, including many twelfth century churches, with their special ancient 'black Virgins', there is still the Aubrac Plateau on the southern boundary, rolling and turning across a landscape of long grasses and secret woodlands – with snow that may stay till May (as also happens further north), to be followed by white crocus and narcissus, which appear secretly with the south wind.

Food: Limousin specialises in pâté de foie gras stuffed with black truffles. Chestnuts, from the extensive woodlands, are used throughout the cuisine. Petit ventres (ewes' paunch, stuffed). Brejaude (cabbage and bacon soup). Girau (sausage). Farcidures (meat and potato balls). Cherry clafoutis, Galette corrézienne (chestnut and walnut tart). Curd cheese (caillade).

All over Auvergne you will be offered aligot, a simple filling dish of mashed potatoes mixed with cheese, baked or fried with bacon and garlic. Broccana, sausage meat and veal pâté. Friand de St Flour. Sausage meat wrapped in pastry. Gigot broyande, leg of lamb braised in white wine, with vegetables and herbs.
Cheese: Bleu d' Auvergne, commercial but very good. Cantal or Fourme de Salers, Chambérat.
Wines: No great vineyards here, but similar to those from the Loire, which are made from Sauvignon Blanc and Chardonnay grapes. In the far south Entraygues, Estaing and Marcillac produce dry whites and red.
Départements: Limousin-Corrèze, Creuse, Haute Vienne, Auvergne-Allier, Cantal, Haute-Loire, Puy de Dôme.
Principal towns and cities: Aurillac, Aubusson, Clermont-Ferrand, Le Puy, Limoges, Royat, St Flour, Vichy.

Along the Loire
The heart of France is appropriately named 'Centre-Val de Loire', and it, together with the Pays de Loire to the west, claims

more important cities, university towns and historic chateaux than any other region. For all that, despite two atomic power stations, great slate quarries and burgeoning local industries, much of the essential country of the Loire riverside is fundamentally unspoiled, though tourism, a necessary industry for many of its inhabitants, takes its toll with the usual vulgarisation of notices and advertisements, although not so brash as in many other places.

Begin by travelling upstream from Nantes, once the capital of Brittany, and now a part of the Loire Atlantique. Lovers of this city complain that improvements designed to facilitate traffic circulation (even the various arms of the river are now underground) have spoilt the picturesque quality but there is still plenty to see, a castle full of museums, a cathedral, and so on.

The Loire itself does not appear in all its glory until you leave the city behind, and the first sight of that broad expanse and silver light under an immense blue sky decorated with scudding clouds is enough to make the most unromantic house hunter feel that he should look no further for a region to which he could give his heart. And so, onwards, to Angers, the former capital of Anjou, which confuses the stranger by being on the rivers Maine and Sarthe, leaving the Loire to glide silently by to the south. The *château* here has that wonderful tapestry of the Apocalypse dating from 1375, and there is an unusual herb garden, high on the ramparts, from which to get an excellent view, both of the *château* itself and of the spreading town.

As centre of the important Anjou wine trade, with a fair every January, Angers typifies the wide cultural and commercial attractions of this region, reflected again and again in the broad sweeps of the mighty river. The natural beauties of the valley, its vine-clad slopes, arable fields, and great mixed forests bestow a peacefulness that is very hard to equal elsewhere; and once he is on the spot, the first-time visitor understands very well why the kings of France and the great merchant princes chose this particular corner for the construction of their splendid *châteaux*.

In the past twenty years or so modern civilisation has been able to make full use of this wonderful background; the fortunate residents have a galaxy of entertainment year round, with every kind of exhibition, festival, plus historical *son et lumière* performances.

Mild weather has endowed much of the valley with a Mediterranean vegetation, and along the central reaches known as the Touraine, market gardens and tree nurseries have come into their own. Mushrooms grow in extensive caves that burrow in the hills a little to the south.

It is difficult to understand why this wide countryside with its interesting background and agreeable climate has not been more sought after by the French themselves for *résidences secondaires*, but it almost certainly has something to do with summer temperatures. On the whole the French like to bake, immerse themselves in oceans or utilise their country homes for *sports d'hiver*. Here, unless the proximity of 1992 has already heralded a last-minute change, you will still find little farms and deserted *chartreuses* with their '*A Vendre*' notices in worn paint, and invariably of handcut local 'tufa' (the cream-coloured stone which brightens into white as time advances). Roofs may be of grey slate, pink/red flat tiles or semi-pantiled.

As well as the advantage of finding old houses still, there is the great benefit of local vineyards which produce wine that is at its best when drunk 'young' and at a fraction of the cost of the 'great' vintages.

Tours, capital of the Touraine, an old university city and proud of speaking 'the purest French in the country', has preserved much of its past, despite disastrous damage during the last war, and deserves a second look from all those who appreciate urban brilliance in an antique setting. Although there are new housing developments, large blocks of flats and neat houses with gardens, further south near the River Cher, from time to time *appartements* must also be available in the middle of the ancient ecclesiastical city, perhaps near historic Place Plumereau with its half-timbered houses, only a short walk from the excellent shopping area. To belong to this place – to stroll past its old mansions, explore the chateau-decorated country and take part in the many cultural activities – would be a delight in itself. Orléans, suffering equally with Tours, has been well restored, but despite the illogical English passion for Joan of Arc, does not capture the imagination in the same way.

Blois, lying in between, almost entirely on the northern bank, has nearly doubled its population in the past thirty years. As the business centre of a large farming area and with a steadily growing *centre commercial*, almost a satellite, to the north, it is a great magnet for job seekers in many different walks of life. At Blois the majesty of the river is outstanding. For nearly two thousand years it was an important means of communication, but the coming of the railways signed its death warrant. By that time the amount of dredging necessary to maintain a deep channel has become extremely difficult, and when it was more or less abandoned, the gravel banks became quickly impassable. In early spring, after the wet season, you can glimpse its former glories; a controversial plan exists to dredge the Loire again and make it navigable once more.

The tributary countries also enjoy wide peaceful skies, and the extraordinary leisurely feeling mirrors the past, rather than the primarily industrial present that France is now pursuing. Although the smaller landscapes have a similar contentment, their valleys are apt to be more secret, tree-grown, and more deeply hidden by banks, but they, too, are great rivers in their own right, the Cher runs for 219 miles (352km) before feeding the Loire; the Indre, 166 miles (267km); the 'little Loir' (without an 'e') runs 194 miles (312km) to the Sarthe, which then, in its turn, becomes the Maine before it, too, reaches the Loire.

Last but not least, there are the two greatest cathedral cities of France – Chartres, to the west, though more properly considered as being in the environs of Paris – and Bourges, to the east. Chartres, on the left bank of the River Eure, beckons for many miles across the featureless plain of La Beauce with its great wheat farms (although there is also a pretty, almost secret, valley). Its incomparable Gothic cathedral is surrounded by old houses, a conservation area and restricted traffic circulation along narrow lanes lined with interesting shops. 'Greater Chartres' has become something of a dormitory for Paris, and you are unlikely to find house bargains. However, retired amateurs or architecture might find the ambience and tone and culture here infinitely preferable to the competitive life in Paris, only 57 miles (88km) away. There are several new suburbs to the west of the town.

The valleys of the Eure are worth exploring. Small pockets of woodland, reclaimed marshes and gravel pits which have turned into lakes, provide many a residential oasis.

Bourges, to explorers by map, seems a far cry from Nantes, where our trip along the river began. It is actually on the River

Yèvre, a tributary of the Cher, and is only an hour away from the delightful central stretch of that river which terminates soon after the very beautiful *château* of Chenonceaux. Once the capital of Berry, it is now capital of the Cher *département*. Famous for the widest Gothic cathedral in the world, Bourges has the most wonderful stained glass anywhere. That great expert on the Loire, Vivian Rowe, called the 'first sight of Saint Etienne at Bourges a great religious and emotional experience felt as deeply by the unbeliever as by the believer', and if I were given free choice of all the cathedral cities in the world, this is certainly the one I should choose. As well as the cathedral, there is the fine mansion that belonged to Jacques Coeur in 1400, and there are also winding streets with many old timbered houses.

It is a pity that the plain surrounding Bourges is not attractive. The beauties of the Cher and Loire have departed – or perhaps the contrast is suddenly too great?

Food: baked pike and stuffed carp from along the Loire. Stuffed bream from Maine and Loire, and sorrel flavoured Chad. Poulet en barbouille – chicken in a blood thickened wine sauce. Venison cutlets in autumn.
Port Salut cheese from the Abbey of that name. Bleu de Touraine and goat's cheese everywhere.
Wine: local wines almost everywhere, inexpensive and good drunk young. Muscadet from Loire Maritime and Maine et Loire. From Cher, a special favourite, the white Sancerre; for inexpensive drinking the white wines of Tannoy, and the reds: Sagoule, La Charite and Cosme. The Coteaux du Layon is a luscious dessert wine, and Saumur's Mousseux is a cheap alternative to Champagne.
Départements: Cher, Eure et Loir, Indre, Indre et Loire, Loir et Cher, Loiret, Loire Atlantique, Maine-et-Loire. (Western Loire is actually in a separate political region: it adds three *départements* to the list. Unfortunately we have had to neglect these here – Mayenne and Sarthe, in the north, which to most travellers always seem to belong to Normandy, and the region south of Nantes, which we have just glanced at above, interesting old Vendée.
Principal towns and cities: Angers, Blois, Chartres, Bourges, Le Mans, Nantes, Orleans, Tours.

Burgundy

If you could fly in a balloon over just two or three provinces, this surely would be included in your list. Guidebooks are apt to complain that this region has no natural frontiers; that it is elusive and difficult to describe. The region has a cultural unity that springs from pride in the past and appreciation of the unspoilt walled towns and villages where so many *châteaux*, abbeys and churches survive.

To the stranger Burgundy means wine, and it comes as a surprise that only 10 per cent of the agricultural production is given over to vineyards – the most important of these checkerboard slopes are celebrated at the end of our exploration. Outside of Dijon, 25 per cent of all Burgundians are engaged in agriculture. Sens must be our first objective, where in the Middle Ages the Archbishop was one of the most important men in France. Then, after Auxerre, one of the oldest towns in France (where the abbey Church of St Germain has the earliest frescoes – ninth century), we shall follow the Chablis winefields before making a circuit of many *châteaux*, among which Tanlay and Ancy-le-Franc prove particularly seductive. This mixture goes on and on, the peaceful, mellow, well cultivated countryside and splendid buildings each needing close attention, while one marvels at the extraordinary lack of brash modern developments, particularly in places like Vézelay, where the Basilica of Mary Magdalene still crowns the hillside, decorated only with a curving street of ancient houses.

Dijon, the historic capital, also preserves the past, though it now marches with the times and has had to accept new suburbs and industrial estates. Between 1360 and 1477, the four Valois dukes who ruled here owned land from Holland in the north to as far south as Provence, and the legacy of this period remains in the city, where there are good Renaissance houses and an imposing ducal palace housing the Fine Arts Museum. Almost due west the wooded highlands of the Morvan, a Celtic word for 'Black Mountain' break up the landscape. The famous Côte D'Or vineyards lie to the south. These 'Golden Hills' are home to the great wines, a prosperous area of good stone houses with cellars, and *châteaux* such as the Clos de Vougeot.

At Beaune, the renowned Hotel-Dieu, that rare Gothic hospital with famous lozenged roofs, rivals even the most renowned appellations. This institution auctions its own wine to provide income both for the Hotel-Dieu, which is now a long-stay hospital for old people, and for the town's medical services. To the south west you will find one of Burgundy's great towns, Autun, with well preserved Roman gates and other remains. The medieval ramparts give good views of the Morvan hills, which in some places rise to more than 2,950ft (900m). Further south still lies the Cluny Romanesque Abbey, but little more than the cloister remains. It was ransacked in the Wars of Religion and suppressed in the Revolution. Remnants of its great library still exist, but once it was larger than any in Christendom. Today, people come this way to see the national stud, one of the twenty-two in France.

You can safely say that the best of everything edible grows and grazes in Burgundy, and you will notice particularly the handsome white Charolais cattle, now selling abroad as well as producing the best beef in France, as they have done for centuries. The summer fields brilliant with yellow flowers advertise the great mustard of Dijon, introduced into Gaul by the Romans.

Food: Burgundians will tell you quite unashamedly that theirs is by far the best food in France, and perhaps it is! Some call it the most sumptuous of country cooking; others believe it is the highest of Haute Cuisine. Those who are 'in the know' say that the really superb restaurants are those between the Côte D'Or and the Mâconnais to the south, on the principle that the best wine tends to produce the best food. (And we mustn't forget that the people around Lyon certainly think the same.)
Here the two authentic Burgundian dishes, coq au vin and boeuf bourgignon, in wine sauce, are brought to perfection. Civet de lièvre (jugged hare) is stewed in wine. Freshwater crayfish from the Morvan, gratinée. Snails with Burgundian stuffing.
As many as three hundred different cheeses include Soumaintrain, Charollais, Chevreton de Mâcon and Montrachet.
Wine: The rather complex system of classifying wines in Burgundy will not really confuse you since the 'great' wines also happen to be some of the most expensive wines in the world. However, before laying down crates at vast expense, it is probably necessary to check that you really are acquiring the *Grand Crus*. These are all grown in the Côte D'Or, reached by the N.74. The Côte de Nuits produce the rich red Burgundies; Côte de Beaune,

red and white. Chablis, from the north, though dry, is fruity and very costly – AC Petit Chablis is a good substitute. All wines labelled AC Bourgogne are made from the same grape type as the great wines. *Marc*, distilled from the grape residue of wine making, is the traditional brandy of Burgundy. *Fine* is produced like cognac, from wine.

Départements: Côte D'Or, Nievre, Saône-et-Loire, Yonne.

Principal towns and cities: Auxerre, Beaune, Dijon, Nevers, Chalon-sur-Saône.

In the North
Brittany and Normandy

Ancient ethnic ties and long historical connections link us to these neighbouring provinces which, oddly enough, are closer to us in many ways than they are to each other.

People in Brittany seem to find an enduring kinship in our common name. Normans, having largely forgotten that they once ruled our country, remark on our common geography – the similarity of beechwoods on chalk, cornfields, and the apple orchards and half timbered houses of Kent and Sussex.

Bretons, as passionate individualists, are actually nearer the Welsh and Cornish than any of the French, their ancestors, the Celts, having arrived from Britain when they were driven out by the Saxons in AD 460. These people renamed the old land of Armor, which had been chosen by the Gauls. Subjugated by Charlemagne in 799, Brittany in fact remained an independent duchy for centuries until 1532. Two hundred years ago the inhabitants of Cornwall and of south Brittany probably understood each other perfectly, but though Cornish is now almost a dead language, Breton can still be learned in French secondary schools, although French is the common tongue of the peninsula. First time visitors are always intrigued by the identical place names in Cornwall and in Morbihan, which is on the south coast, or Basse Bretagne.

Between the two world wars, the attractive national costume with lace coifs and black dresses was common in many districts; nowadays, apart from some head-dresses, they are seen mostly at festivals. What is known as 'regionalism' is very active, with more and more Celtic clubs reviving customs, and politically minded people supporting some kind of longed-for independence that is very unlikely to come about. But despite traditional leanings, Brittany has made almost more consistent efforts to live in the twentieth century than any other province.

It must be at least twenty or thirty years since many communities were rehoused in neat white cottages with slate roofs in place of the older granite dwellings, and these snug villages have expanded to include sizeable developments of *résidences secondaires*. Greatly improved roads have replaced the narrow, picturesque lanes connecting seaside villages. But it is at the sea, for so long the economic background of the average Breton family, that one discovers the full individuality of this rugged peninsula, so different both from Normandy and the shores further south. The deeply cut, sea-eroded and sea-sculpted coast running for 600 miles (965km) and much worked on by the great tides, was known as Armor, 'land of the sea'. Inland was Argoat, 'land of the woods'. Now it is mostly scrub with pleasant wooded valleys in between.

As one travels west along the Armor coast, low granite cliffs separate sandy bays, and seascapes further west display strange pink rocks in every conceivable size. The attractive port of Roscoff ushers in some fine sandy beaches until deep indentations take over again, and in the far west you meet Finistère, where the Atlantic gales have for centuries decimated the ships of the sea-girt community.

Inland you will discover the extraordinary parish closes – carved triumphal arches, Calvaries and statuary, grouped around the small squares at the side of a church – striking religious survivals from the seventeenth century. The Breton *pardons*, processions in regional costumes, with a deeply religious significance, are another aspect of the devotional nature of the people. A circuit of the parish closes takes in the Arrée Mountains, the highest part of Brittany, although the altitude is no more than 1,310ft (400m).

Rounding the point, and leaving the most violent storms of the Atlantic behind, you come to Quimper, Brittany's one-time capital, with fifteenth century houses and a splendid twin-spired cathedral. And here folklore reaches its height when the biggest folk festival in Europe is held in July. The former Bishop's Palace houses a folklore museum and Breton costumes. To many parts of the south west coast below here all the way round to Morbihan in Basse Bretagne, came the first British family holidaymakers between the wars, and you will find yourself at home in the little resorts.

Further east again is the extraordinary concentration of pre-historic megaliths around Carnac – thousands of 'great stones' set up between 5,000 and 2,000 BC, a mixture of cromlechs, dolmens (or passage graves) and innumerable parallel lines – the *Alignements du Menac et Kermario*, some of them similar to the lines on Dartmoor, and others like Avebury.

In this part of Brittany, particularly, the influence of the Gulf Stream brings soft, warm weather, and if you travel north east across the country, you skirt La Ceinture D'Orée, or Golden Belt, of prosperous market gardens. This climate is shared with the resort of La Baule which, as well as being fashionable, has great charm – a beautiful bay of sand, massed flowers, and the shelter of pine trees.

Those other distant cousins of ours across the Channel, the Normans, are descended from Scandinavian pirates who sailed up the River Seine in the ninth century, looting and burning and exhibiting a trial of strength. In 911 Charles the Frank made terms with their leader, Rolf (later to be known as Rollo), who then became 'Dux ', or first Duke, in the land eventually known as Normandy (which was actually two thirds of the ancient terri-tory of Neustria that had come into being under Clovis, first king of the Franks). Rollo was baptised and made reparation for what he had destroyed, building churches and monasteries throughout the remainder of his life. One hundred and fifty-five years later, William the Bastard set sail for England and changed the entire pattern of the medieval world.

In Normandy, the countryside has an air of long settled and prosperous civilisation, and the richness and variety has depended on a cohesion between the sea and land communities. The white chalk cliffs of Ault Onival is what is known as Upper Normandy, to the north, match the Eastbourne cliffs across the Channel, but the River Bresle breaks up the high land at Le Tréport and Mers-les-Bains, and this alternation of cliffs and small resorts, more rural in character than the average English town, continues all the way to Le Havre. Dieppe, with the most attractive passenger port anywhere, is holding its own in the dif-ficult world of ferries. Its services, having been disturbed by many strikes when owned jointly by Sealink and French Railways, are now solely in the hands of the French. Dieppe has appeal as a first-class shopping centre for a large area, partly because of excellent parking near the attractively pedestrianised precinct behind the esplanade. Fécamp's importance as a port for codfish has doubt-less held its own because of the greatly increased consumption of fish in France since the price of meat began to hit a new high after the petrol crisis. An enlarged yacht basin helps its difficult bid towards genuine resort status.

Redeveloped Le Havre is the principal container port of northern France and is flanked by petro-chemical installations, which bring prosperity along with undoubted spoliation of both the land and luminious skies that once so powerfully attracted the Impressionist painters.

What you might call the spirit of Normandy is found along the Seine estuary (where shipping can still penetrate as far as Rouen) and through the Seine Valley, made bright twice yearly in spring and autumn by the cherry trees, beechwoods and apple orchards. Rouen, capital of Upper Normandy, is, taken as a whole, the most attractive city in northern France, with hilly suburbs on the north eastern flank, and the River Seine enclosing it on two sides. It is liable to be underappreciated by first time visitors because the approach is so dilapidated, and traffic circulation can be difficult, but with more than its full share of excellent galleries, and its restored cathedral and churches, there is a rich reward for admirers of flamboyant Gothic and of half timbered houses from the Middle Ages. Though so far inland, it is the fourth largest port of France, loading more grain than any other, and to stand on its central bridge over the Seine, with busy shipping to the fore, and city spires behind, can be a heart-stopping moment.

The grain that arrives comes mostly from the great Norman farms south of the river. The Caux region to the north is a pre-dominantly mixed agricultural area, with flax and beet grown widely. Both cattle and horses are raised, but milk is the main source of income.

The Calvados coast from Honfleur to Grandcamp, aptly named La Côte Fleurie, with its sands and low cliffs, has the lovely old medieval port of Honfleur and some pleasant resorts – popular Trouville and its twin, the star Deauville, a glittering, fashion-able resort with two racecourses, regattas, polo matches, etc. The landing beaches of the historic Normandy offensive, D-Day, are met further west.

Pleasant residential suburbs are still being built at the restored city of Caen, capital of Lower Normandy, which was much devastated during the last war. Chosen by William the Conqueror as his ducal seat, and with its *château* and two great abbeys miraculously conserved, the city has wide avenues and splendid new buildings faced with local stone, a triumph for post-war planners. The little port of Ouistreham has been deepened to take larger ships able to deal with its increasing success in industry, and provide a new ferry crossing. Here again are extensive residential developments. Many Parisians have *résidences secondaires*, either flats or villas along this coast.

Near Bayeux, where the famous tapestry is brilliantly displayed, and Falaise, where William was born, are the last keys to the necessary history of the region. Between these two towns lie pleasantly wooded valleys locally called Suisse Normande. Though not at all majestic, there is an alpine air in the sunken valleys and quickly running stream of the River Orne. Apple orchards for cider and the liqueur Calvados are found extensively throughout this *bocage* (open woodland) of the south. There is some new development in what could become a dormitory area for Caen.

Thoroughbred race horses and saddle horses are bred to the east, in the Pays d'Auge and around Argentan. St Lo, on the River Vire, another charming, wooded region east of the Cotentin Peninsula, holds a famous horse sale each September. The renowned St Lo stud may be visited. The wonderful wild coastal scenery below the port of Cherbourg now has a new neighbour in the form of a nuclear power station (which does not appear on many tourist maps). Around a vast estuary encircling the extraordinary Mont St Michel, the weather again is distinctly warmed by the Gulf Stream.

Housing styles vary considerably from north to south, but whether in brick or stone, most houses have slate roofs. It is a pity that the typical small Norman farms and the old half timbered barns are scarcely echoed in the latest building developments.

In the Normandy-Maine regional national park, created in 1975, 575,240 acres (232,972ha) between Bagnoles-de-L'Orne and Alençon in the south of the province, spread out across five forests, and are devoted to the protection of rural life through the development of agriculture, crafts, tourism and sport.

Food: Cream sauce is a hallmark of Norman cooking, for both poultry and fish. Demoiselles are baby lobsters from Cherbourg. Tripe is a speciality of Caen, with recipes dating back to the fourteenth century. Unsalted Normandy butter can be a daily luxury backing up the historic cheeses, Pont L'Evêque, from the thirteenth century and Livarot and Camembert (eighteenth century). The white Breton chicken (poulet blanc breton), which is ready for eating at twelve weeks, is almost entirely free range. Boudins blancs and noirs come from Rennes (white and black pudding).

Cider: What Normandy lacks in vines it makes up for with a wide choice of cider – sparkling, cidre bouché, or dry (brut/sec) or sweet (doux). Perry, a 'cider' made from pears, is also obtainable. Calvados – liqueur cider – or 'brandy' – is a smooth drink after it has aged for fifteen years. Bénédictine, a sweet liqueur from Fécamp, was invented by a monk in 1510.

Départements: (Norman) Calvados, Eure, Manche, Orne, Seine Maritime. (Breton) Côtes du Nord, Finistère, Ile et Vilaine,. Morbihan.

Principal towns and cities: (Norman) Caen, Cherbourg, Le Havre, Rouen. (Breton) Brest, Nantes, Quimper, Rennes, St Malo.

The North East

Various drawbacks have kept foreigners away from semipermanent settlement in this area, and it makes sense to examine the similarities and diversities of Alsace, Lorraine and Vosges together.

Alsace lies parallel to Lorraine, in the north, abutting the Rhine, and is altogether flatter. The northern part of Lorraine is industrial, but the fine wooded hills of the Vosges, still with their timber trade, lie between the two. It is rewarding to explore the Moselle river linking Metz and Nancy, for Nancy has been called the most elegant provincial town in Western Europe. Actually, lovers of architecture will find it most inspiring, a real centre of art and culture, inherited from the time of Stanislas, the deposed King of Poland who was son-in-law of Louix XV. For an industrialist it could be a very acceptable background in which to raise a family with artistic leanings.

Alsace Lorraine was only re-attached to France in 1945, having been annexed by Germany three times in the previous eighty years. Many farmers actually emigrated to Algeria between 1870 and 1918, and their descendants returned in 1966. Members of old Alsace families will tell you of their 'confusion' at having been French at one time of their lives, German at another, and then French again, but the uneasiness of this is dropping into the past. Strasbourg is justly regarded as one of France's most attractive cities, and it also serves its rich industrial area (iron and coal) with great ability. It is the only French city on the Rhine. Ancient houses, a vast cathedral and good museums all fit in with its reputation as an educational centre, but the old atmosphere has been somewhat eclipsed by its new role as seat of the Council of Europe and the European Parliament, and all that the new cosmopolitan inhabitants bring with them.

Despite positive trends, general unemployment has already forced many Alsacians to seek their fortunes in Switzerland. Here they enjoy a special status as *travailleurs frontaliers*, which means they reside in France and commute to Switzerland on a daily or weekly basis. The extreme climate of Alsace benefits from the shelter given by the Vosges, and it is the sunniest corner of north east France. Even tobacco is grown. The many miles of vineyards, and the mixed cultivation of fruit and vegetables, have been changed minimally by industrialisation. The villages have a picture book quality, completed by storks' nests.

The heavy industries of Lorraine were developed by German investment between 1870 and 1918, and their decline has only partially been made good by the development of the petro-chemical industry. However, south of the iron and steel centres around Thionville, are wide fields and fertile plains; and in the somewhat severe climate, freezing in winter and scorching in summer, cherry and plum trees are cultivated for a profitable production of *Kirsch*, *mirabelle* and *quetsch*. Further south still come the mineral springs which produce *Vittel* and *Contrexéville* (the cheapest bottled mineral waters), and the growing fashion for health cures is also revitalising old resorts like Vittel and Bains-les-Bains.

In fact, the harshest winter conditions in the whole of France are to be found in Vosges, where a recent money-spinner is ski-de-fond (cross-country skiing) as well as downhill skiing, a form of tourism that fits in very well with the traditional dairy farming and linen production. In summer more and more tourists visit both Vosges and Alsace to follow the long established Route du Vin, visiting picturesque villages like Riquewihr, where the Riesling vineyards come right up to the old walls, and Obernai, which has a thirteenth century belfry and a famous fountain. This expansion in both winter and summer tourism is providing a much needed source of income.

Food: (Alsace) - German influence here produces sauerkraut, boudin noir (black pudding), knackwurst (small frankfurter-type sausage), saucisse de Strasbourg (smoked pork and beef sausage). (*Lorraine*) - quiche Lorraine containing egg custard and bacon, potée Lorraine (pork stew with bacon and vegetables), tourte à la Lorraine (pork and veal cream tart). *Vosges* - pork chops cooked with wine and plums.
Wines: Riesling, Gewürztraminer, Muscat, Sylvaner, Pinot Blanc are all famous. Crémant d'Alsace is sparkling. Drink most Alsace wines young but Tokay d'Alsace needs some years in the bottle. Liqueurs include the well-known Framboise, Mirabelle, Quetsch, Kirsch, Mûre, Myrtille, Reine Claude, and a rare one, Houx (Holly).
Strasbourg, Champigneulles, Metz and Schitligheim produce good light beer.
Départements: Bas-Rhin, Haut-Rhin, Meurthe-et-Moselle, Meuse, Moselle, Vosges.
Principal towns and cities: Nancy, Metz, Colmar, Epinal, Lunéville, Ribeauvillé, Strasbourg, Verdun, Vittel.

The Ardennes and Champagne
It was to be expected that this lightning tour of France could not be confined to more or less neat geographical areas the further north we travelled, so this section is concerned primarily with the economic region that was founded in the 1960s. Study of the map of *départements* shows that Champagne-Ardennes has been squeezed in between Burgundy and Alsace Lorraine, Ile de France and Nord, and any attempt at a proper geographical division would push the forest region of Ardennes into Belgium and award Champagne to Burgundy (which is already large enough).

France's oldest forest is the *Arduenna Sylva* of Caesar, which 2,000 years ago stretched as far as the Rhine. The Ardennes as a whole lie in France, Belgium and Luxembourg – in Celtic this word means 'deep forest'. Linked with the German Eifel area, it has for some years been developing as a European 'holiday region without frontiers'. Perhaps because the 'continental' climate brings dry weather in spring and autumn, the largely deciduous woodlands have been described as the best walking country in northern France, and exceptionally fine autumn colours combined with long-distance footpaths, and 370 miles (600km) of towpath walking, attract both residents and visitors. There are some celebrated river views and two gems: one of the largest castles in Europe, at Sedan, built to hold 7,000 men, and the splendid royal square of the Place Ducale (1610), at Charleville-Mézières, originally two towns built within two loops of the River Meuse. Once nails and cannon balls came from here. Now it is the centre of French precision metallurgy. On a smaller scale are the little iron foundries that exist here and there at the forest edge along with craftsmen who have preserved basketware, weaving, etc. (There is also a special 'Sedan stitch' carpet.)

Many ancient legends and historical stories from the time of Charlemagne are intertwined with the winding of the River Meuse, and a leisurely trip may be taken from Monthermé between the great woods that tower up more than a thousand feet (over 300m). This reach of the river was for a long time quite unknown to ordinary people, being mainly the preserve of barge owners, and the pursuit of tourism as a necessary money spinner has benefited both residents and visitors.

Not only the Meuse now welcomes the boats; Champagne-Ardennes as a whole is turning into a genuine 'Lake District'. Charleville-Mézières has a leisure centre, the Lac des Vieilles Forges, where motorised craft are banned, and windsurfers and small dinghy enthusiasts can tack to their hearts' content. Further south are two large manmade lakes. One, 6,000 acres (2,430 ha) in extent, the Lac de la Forêt d'Orient, was created in 1966 to check the flow of the Seine. This is exceedingly popular with residents of Paris and Troyes. On one side of the lake is an ornithological reserve of 740 acres (300 ha), where access is forbidden and wildlife protected. The common crane is an important migrant. Many species of birds that are rare in the region also use the lake.

The Lac du Der-Chantecoq (12,000 acres/4,860ha) east of Troyes in the Bocage Champenois is said to be the largest manmade water in Europe; 1,500 acres (607 ha) are set aside for water ski-ing and parts have been constructed for dinghies and motorised craft. One of the most agreeable aspects of the scheme is the participation of local people who have organised a society known as the Amis du Lac so that regular users of the lake can get to know the local inhabitants.

Troyes is the capital of the Aube *département*, a rather flat wheat-growing area, and although now an industrial centre, it has preserved its old town with lanes and alleyways between gabled houses, and many churches. The Gothic cathedral has an outstanding 'Treasure', though much of the interior was damaged in the Revolution; there is splendid stained glass, some dating back to the thirteenth century.

Four more lakes have been created around Langres, in the south. In this countryside can be found very low priced '*fermettes* ' and one-storey chalets that have even reached as far as Troyes, more or less linking the whole area. Langres was an independent Gaulish town when the Romans arrived and still carries on business within 2½ miles (4km) of ramparts. Standing high on the edge of a plateau, it is one of the northern gateways to Burgundy just south of pleasant undulating country to the west of the River Marne. You can follow the river from here, 120 miles (nearly 200km), to Chalôns-sur-Marne, where you will begin to see the actual vineyards of Champagne.

It is said that the vines that produce champagne prosper particularly on the solid chalk which lies beneath the regional *Parc* known as the Montagne de Reims, between Reims and Epernay. Epernay, on the Marne, has been sacked and burned so many times throughout its history that it has nothing to show other than the comfortable buildings of its champagne barons. Here, at a constant temperature of between 10 and 12°C (50 and 54°F) are 62 miles (100km) of champagne cellars in the chalk subsoil. Guided tours are available for visitors, as they also are in Reims. Clovis, the first Christian king of the Franks, was baptised in Reims Cathedral and most of the succeeding kings were crowned in the same building; in the space of 700 years it was pulled down and rebuilt frequently. Today's Gothic cathedral from 1428 is exceptionally fine, and there are other good churches together with one of the leading fine arts museums in France. Charming, undulating countryside leads to the Benedictine Monastery of Hautvilliers, where Dom Pérignon first put the sparkle into a blended wine in 1670.

Food: Champagne matches its sparkling wine with Haute Cuisine, similar to adjoining Ile de France, and also borrows from Burgundy its good beef dishes – boeuf à la bourguignonne and boeuf à la mode. Andouillettes spread right across the north. Pâtés and terrines are wrapped in pastry at Reims. Fresh water fish. Its own cheeses include: Caprice des Dieux, Cendré de Champagne, Chaource, Chaumont and Langres.

The Ardennes dishes borrow from Belgium first class charcuterie, roast venison and wild boar, game pies and pâtés.

Wines: Top champagne, Krug, Bollinger or Taittinger, are today followed very closely by Mumm, Laurent-Perrier and many others. Small growers, with much cheaper productions, are worth research. A still white wine, Côteaux Champenois, and local red wines are drunk young.

Départements: Ardennes, Aube, Marne, Haute Marne.

Principal towns and cities: Châlons-sur-Marne, Charleville-Mézières, Chaumont, Epernay, Langres, Reims, Troyes.

Picardie, Artois and Flanders

You would be wrong to assume that the north of France is not worthy of a long stay simply because some people say that the weather is the same as in Britain, the countryside has been devastated by two world wars and there's no wine produced locally. For the energetic who have good jobs, for students studying specialities such as art and architecture, and for the semi-retired who like food and wine (which, after all, need not be grown on the spot) and who need to return reasonably easily to the UK, the north can provide conditions that are not easily matched by the English Home Counties a mere 40 miles (64km) away.

Three quite different regions making up the old provinces of Picardie, Artois and Flanders – the latter two now being administered under the label of Nord-Pas de Calais – confuse the casual visitor. These are the old Black Country of coal mines and mining villages, now joined by the petro-chemical and paint industries, restricted to an area near Belgium some 50 miles (80km) long and running east/west to the south of Lille, principally between St Amand-les-Eaux and Béthune. Then there is the prosperous farmland, lightly wooded here and there, stretching to the North Sea, and interspersed with reclaimed, productive marshland, and, finally the sand-girt riband of large and small resorts.

A surprisingly high number of listed buildings are in this relatively small region, where great squares, ancient houses and tall belfries with melodious chimes, have managed to survive two major conflicts. And as many as six cathedrals, which include the great Amiens – regarded as the most perfect example of northern Gothic in the whole of France – still stand in towns ravaged by the 1940 bombardments.

The number of wooded areas is also surprising, so that some distance south of the largely rebuilt industrial town of Maubeuge you can find first the Avesnois, with its pastures, forests and valleys, and then, on the way to Laon, to the Thiérache, a land of dairies and cider orchards. The rebuilding in battle-torn areas has mostly been so thorough that it is difficult to grasp the terrible extent of the fighting which took place in the two world wars. Only the extensive cemeteries serve as reminders.

Expatriates obliged to work in Nord as part of a long-term employment agreement could profitably investigate the housing situation in the surprising city of Lille, fifth largest in France, and now classified by the French as a town of special artistic interest. Some lovely old buildings combine with particularly generous areas of open space. With one million inhabitants (42 per cent of whom are under twenty-five) it is, naturally, both energetic and noisy. Together with its satellites of Roubaix and Tourcoing, it is regarded as one of the great textile centres of the world, and certainly the most important economic centre of northern France, manufacturing everything from biscuits to turbines. And it now has a Métro to ease transport in the centre.

For too long Calais has tended to be a place people rushed through, bound for sunnier spots. Now, far-seeing Europeans are buying properties in the rolling hinterland, charmed by some surprisingly pretty small stretches of wooded countryside, the pantiled, extremely reasonably priced, one-storeyed cottages of old Flanders, and the ease and speed with which one can be reconnected to the UK. Prices have not yet inflated here, and the proximity of good sandy shores could make a speculative investment attractive. Between Sangatte and Ambleteuse the cliff-backed shoreline is designated as an area of outstanding natural beauty.

It has been assumed that the opening of the Channel Tunnel in 1995 will bring all sorts of jobs for the British, though there is no reason to suppose that the French will not organise these thoroughly and efficiently, and reserve them for themselves, since the SNCF rightly regard their railway system as one of the best in Europe. Tourist traffic will doubtless increase.

Hilly Boulogne has a good deal more charm than Calais, and the little Edwardian town of Wimereux immediately to the north has been a favourite resort with the British since the opening decade of this century, though the beaches are not quite so sandy as those further north. All along this coast you will find housing developments amid pleasant coastal scenery.

The showplace up here is Le Touquet – Paris-Plage. This fashionable spot holds a lot for the retired person with a really good income, the hotelier with ideas, or for the 'arrived' executive with a new job in Paris. Millionaires' villas with velvety lawns line the road behind the popular shopping centre, and this is the place in which to settle if you've a taste for off-beat medical care and advanced health and beauty treatments sandwiched in between horse racing, gambling, playing tennis, golf or yachting. There is a first class, up-to-the-minute, luxuriously equipped aquatic leisure park, 53,820 sq ft (5,000 sq m) under a glass pyramid, with saunas, solarium, etc, open all the year round. Not to be overlooked here by retired people is the superior library.

The Somme Valley dominates the Picardie coast, attracting visitors to old St. Valery, which is an ancient maritime fortified town with a pleasant atmosphere and a sea wall. Across the estuary, a little to the north of Le Crotoy, lies the Parc Ornithologique de Marquenterre. Started as a private reserve in 1973, and now open to the public, it has been able to influence l'Office de Chasse to create a maritime reserve of 2½ miles (4km) where birds may not be shot. This is a very great triumph in what is fundamentally a popular wild fowling district. An extremely large area of dune, saltmarsh and mud flat could be of intense interest to retired ornithologists, few of whom seem to know about this reserve.

And the weather is not, in fact, identical to that in Britain. 'The Opal Coast' that runs from Dunkerque to Berck-sur-Mer exhibits shining dappled skies where frequent changes in outlook can be relied upon.

Food: Picardie and Artois – herring and mackerel along the coast. Andouilles and andouillettes (pork and tripe sausages) in Arras and Cambrai, terrines and pâtés wrapped in pastry in Amiens. Langue de Valenciennes Lucullus – smoked tongue with foie gras. Frogs, tripe and thick vegetable soups are common. Flanders – potje vleesch, rabbit, veal and chicken terrine. Veau flamande, veal braised with dried apricots, prunes and raisins, waterzooi, chicken or freshwater fish stewed with vegetables in a creamy sauce.
Cheeses: wide choice – Abbaye de Monts de Cats, mild; particularly strong smelling Boulette d'Avesnes; Maroilles and Puant de Lille.
Beer: thirty-seven breweries around Lille and Armentières produce a quarter of the country's beer. Bars serve a good lager-type Kronenbourg from Alsace in small bottles, but supermarkets all over France stock this and Valstar in litre sizes, much more cheaply.
Genièvre is locally produced gin.
Départements: Nord, Pas-de-Calais, Picardie.
Principal towns and cities: Abbeville, Amiens, Arras, Beauvais.

Ile-de-France and Paris
As we draw near the capital, we come at last to the Ile-de-France. This domain of the early kings has two faces. When Balzac said, 'Of all the places I have seen, this is the nearest to Paradise', he was thinking of the great forests and the splendid *châteaux*, feudal castles like Senlis and Pierrefonds, and the royal palaces of Fontainebleau, Versailles and Compiègne. Today these vast treasures, and innumerable other, smaller ones, still exist, miraculous survivals from so many battles. It depends where you enter the region as to whether you immediately think yourself back several centuries, dallying in the small historic towns, walking in the forests, and admiring the scenery along the Seine, once painted by Sisley and Monet, or whether you surprise yourself by being suddenly in one of the five new towns, satellites built in the 1960s as a dormitory and overflow for the capital. The largest of the five is Marne-La-Vallée, due east of Paris, famous

for its spectacular contemporary architecture which is often used in science fiction films, and because it is to be the site of the new Euro Disneyland!

Despite the large new housing districts, the River Marne also meanders through attractive pockets of countryside, and market gardens are dotted about to the south east. The dense suburban developments near Orly Airport to the south, and Charles de Gaulle to the north east, are less fortunate. In the west, near Boulogne-Billancourt, home of Renault Motorworks, there is substantial industry, both light and heavy. And this pattern is repeated in many of the suburbs.

Since this is the most densely populated part of the country, something like ten million people, one fifth of the entire population, live and work in a comparatively small area. But in the pleasant roads along the edge of the many afforested districts, particularly near Rambouillet in the south west, and Fontainebleau in the south east, are all sorts of postwar houses in the 'millionaire villa' category, homes for Parisians who once had large apartments in the most fashionable *arrondissements* and who now enjoy their ease in a sylvan world dotted with surprisingly good and expensive restaurants. Smaller houses and flats to let can also be found in these out-of-town spots (see also chapter 4, *Setting Up House*). Chantilly race course, due north, has been called the most beautiful race course in the world, and the nearby *château*, a nineteenth century reproduction of the original Renaissance building, now houses the famous Condé collection.

L'Isle-Adam in the Oise Valley is a favourite river resort with Parisians, and Enghien-Les-Bains, also on the Oise, is a lakeside spa with both race course and casino.

Paris
It is probably true to claim that no European capital has changed so much as Paris in the last quarter century. Not only has the famous sky line been pierced by inevitable tower blocks but the existence of the great Boulevard Pérepherique (which was constructed to circumnavigate and link the ancient 'gates' of the historic cities of Porte d'Orléans, Porte Versailles, and so on) changes everything.

This engineering feat, designed to solve the problem of traffic flow (and one has to admire and congratulate, however much deploring the necessity), resembles a vast fairground attraction around which one is whirled in less than human comfort, swinging dizzily past edifices of glass, little parks, or famous landmarks like Sacré Coeur, between rapacious streams of traffic which approach far too near, and then advance and fall back again like fearless sword dancers competing for a kill.

Maybe the half-decided, homeless job-taker should steel himself for a double trip around this dramatic merry-go-round, exploring on and off in the tortuous one-way system and investigating the truly unbelievable parking situation before final acceptance. He can then top off his research with a day on the much-admired Métro in the rush hours, and a journey into the anonymous *banlieues*, the outskirts, or suburbs, where more and more genuine Parisians find themselves obliged to live. These old fashioned residents of Paris will tell you all about the ransacking of parked cars, pickpockets on the Métro, and bag snatchers operating from motor scooters, for Paris is just as unsafe as any other big city.

And since we are accustomed to thinking that France is a much emptier country than England, this is the moment to ponder on the fact that some statisticians claim that Greater Paris is infinitely more crowded than London, with 2.4 times as many people to each square mile – certainly this is the excuse for the claim that the Parisians themselves are always in a hurry, brusque and unhelpful, a complaint that is made in the French provinces, rather than by foreigners.

Somewhere behind these facts, figures, and personal experiences, the Paris which people dream about undoubtedly exists. It *is* the Capital of the World, catering for every kind of human satisfaction; it *is* one of the most beautiful cities anywhere, with splendid squares, spectacular views and magnificent art collections, and it *does* still gather together both thinkers and experimentalists in the field of art. And perhaps that's a way of looking at the secret. We are inevitably drawn by its sparkle, but apart from rather short periods of weeks or months, few of us are qualified to become citizens. The very young, the very rich, and those who are genuinely committed to one of the fields of art, letters, or music (and perhaps the world of high finance) are suited for a long, long stay in Paris. The rest must struggle violently to keep heads above water, tempers calm and bank balances intact. Maybe for a couple of years or so we can do all that profitably, and while we do, we may harvest a lifetime of impressions.

Start perhaps, near the centre, on the evocative Pont des Arts, one of the thirty-five bridges over the Seine, built as a footbridge in 1803 so that students at the Ecole des Beaux Arts and members of the Institut de France, could cross directly to the new art museum of the Louvre. The latest excitement here, of course, is the glass pyramid designed by Mr Pei, an American architect, which opened in the spring of 1989. This bridge has been called the Centre of Civilisation, and looking from it towards the Ile de la Cité in the middle of the river, whose early Gallic inhabitants were once called the *Parisii*, you will see the towers and spire of Notre Dame Cathedral. Here climb a spiral stone staircase to look over the bridges and one of the most picturesque of all views. In the pavement before the great West Front is set *Point Zero*, the exact centre of the city, from which all Paris road distances are measured.

It would be superfluous to recommend in detail all the famous sights around this centre. But the wise researcher will make time for three of the most recent: the Pompidou Centre – that modern art museum which almost caused a major national scandal in 1977, the Musée D'Orsay, former railway station and home of late nineteenth century art – full of surprises, and something unexpected, L'Institut du Monde Arabe. This museum at 23 Quai St Bernard is a cultural centre opened only three years ago, and on the top floor you can rest and meditate, or eat. You will never forget the roofscape seen from here.

Food: justly regarded as the gastronomic capital of Europe, with a unique selection of restaurants offering excellent food at far below UK prices. The centre of Haute Cuisine, classic sauces and elaborate recipes. The word 'restaurant' was invented in Paris in 1765. Nouvelle Cuisine moved in a few years ago and has become the sophisticated choice – minute portions, but incredibly delicious and usually unreasonably expensive.

Cheese: Best-Brie, product of Paris, invented a thousand years ago. Many varieties. Feuille de Dreux, and Fontainebleau.

Wines: In Paris restaurants you will be able to buy the best vintages of great wines that are not obtainable in the provinces, and supermarkets will have a good choice of champagne and better *vins de table*.

Beer: *blonde* and *brune* is local, and from Nord.

Départements: the Ile-de-France is made up of Paris and her *Départements* – Essone, Hauts-de-Seine, Seine et Marne, Seine-St Denis, Val-de-Marne, Val-d'Oise, Yvelines.

Towns: many old towns have been absorbed by the Paris conglomeration, but some have kept their individuality and need a special look – Fontainebleau, Meaux, Moret-sur-Loing, Nemours and Provins among them.

3
Advance Research and Formalities

Since the nearest port in France is merely 25 miles (41 km) away, it makes sense to do some thorough advance research before committing oneself to an entirely new lifestyle. Interviews for important jobs carrying one to quite remote territory often take place in London (or perhaps in Paris) and in the difficult labour market of today, it could be a crucial error not to look thoroughly into the background before acceptance.

Opportunities for full length educational courses also need to be examined. Some of the oldest universities – Aix-en-Provence, Grenoble, Lyon, Montpellier, Toulouse – are in the south, usually referred to as the Midi (an abbreviation of *meridional* – southern). Here summers will be scorching or, as in the case of Grenoble, there may be a freezing winter (which might be preferred for the ski-ing). Newer, '*jeunes* ' universities will also have their points – first rate facilities for scientific research, comfortable halls of residence – lakes or rivers nearby, or even the sea for water sports, and so on. Such details need looking into where a genuine choice exists.

A survey conducted by the newspaper *Le Monde* last year, in its special edition 'Campus' that appears every Tuesday, put the three favourite universities as Rennes, Montpellier and Toulouse, as much for the quality of life in the town as for the cultural outlook. Orsay was the favourite Paris university, and Paris was almost consistently preferred by students from middle class homes (with Lyon, Grenoble, Limoges and Strasbourg as runners up). Students with a working class background were found at Besançon, Grenoble (Stendhal St-Etienne) Metz, Avignon, Lyon and Poitiers.

People looking for retirement homes would appear to be better placed so far as not making mistakes goes, but here again a surprising number of expatriates commit themselves to the purchase of primitive dwellings, requiring much restoration, in regions famous for long, hard winters. There were many heartaches a few years ago when the sudden formidable freeze-up destroyed the *chauffage* – central heating – in hundreds of homes of absentees, as well as in those with bedrooms that were untenanted only for a few days. In the Ardèche, where houses were snowed up and completely cut off, some new inhabitants without heat, and with no means of getting to the shops, eventually took to their beds to wait for the thaw. These major freeze-ups are fortunately rare away from alpine regions, but hard frosts can be just as lethal for unsophisticated plumbing. In the hottest summers, too, completely opposite conditions can be frustrating. A national emergency with a declared state of *sécheresse* in south and central France, quickly brings water regulations into operation, and restrictions naturally affect swimming pool owners, gardeners, etc, so that pools with a built-in need for extravagant water consumption can be a major liability. Although, having said that, swimming pools are generally encouraged as their construction and maintenance creates additional local employment and their existence is welcomed by firemen (*pompiers*) who know that an additional reservoir of water is available in case of fire. All water is metered throughout France, so that 'bending the regulations' is absolutely impossible.

This handful of pointers should be sufficient to underline the need for caution and rather more prudent planning than might at first have been thought necessary.

Travel and Temporary Accommodation

Fortunately, France has never been so easy to explore as it is today. Trains are faster than they have ever been before (see Part II, chapter 8). Autoroutes cut the length of car journeys to a minimum, and hotels, small and large, with an extremely wide price range, are available everywhere. Taking your car across the Channel at short notice can be done without advance booking by carefully selecting an extra early or late crossing on Sealink or P&O (see Appendix B for details; 5-day excursions cut the cost of quick trips).

So many special offers of different kinds exist these days, that it is obviously a wise precaution to pay a personal visit to French Railways, and to the French Government Tourist Office, which are side by side at 178 Piccadilly, London W1V 0AL to look into what is currently available and collect tourist information for preferred regions, picking up some invaluable annual guides,

particularly the current *Traveller in France* with its highly detailed inset covering major formalities, hints on motoring, details
of planes and ferries, consulate addresses, maps and guides, and
so on. Names and addresses of hotel groups are also given. A full
length guide covering the 5,000 family-run hotels of the *Logis* and
Auberges de France, complete with daily rates, is also obtainable
from the French Government Tourist Office on receipt of only 80p
in stamps (1989).

This group of hotels comprises simple *auberges* with rates as
low as 70Fr or 80Fr for a double room (and some even lower),
as well as a range of one, two or three star hotels (with rates
up to 350Fr). The accent is on good cooking, and the smaller
auberges offer phenomenal value for money, since every hotel in
the chain must offer comfortable accommodation consistent with
the standards of tourist hotels, and also guarantee a real welcome
for the guest, with a family flavour. Househunters who settle on
a particular area for in-depth research could take advantage of
demi-pension terms for a long stay, and find themselves very
economically housed, with food included.

Those who prefer a small furnished house or cottage as a
temporary base, could try hiring through the Gîtes de France organisation which can also be contacted at 178 Piccadilly. Typical
weekly rates in the central Indre and Loire region run from 575Fr
(£57) a week (out of season) for a simple house accommodating
five persons, to 695 to 750Fr between June and August. Top rates
are around 1,220 to 1,350Fr (£122 to £135). In fact, hiring a *gite*
temporarily could the answer for those young executives who will
receive a generous housing allowance from their new employers.

Again, the newly retired might think of hiring (or even
buying!) a motor caravan, in order to make a carefree tour
lasting some months, while deciding between different centres.
With the aid of the Michelin *Green Camping and Caravanning
Guide*, small municipal sites open all year round can be located
throughout the country, as well as some luxury establishments
whose winter opening is linked with winter sporting, so that all
facilities – showers, cafés, club rooms etc – are centrally heated.
Research in magazines like *Motor Caravan World.*

Passports and Working Formalities
Within the European Community, there is freedom of movement

for British citizens (and all other nationals of the member states). Originally it was hoped that passports and border controls would be abolished once the Common Market was securely established, but this did not prove to be a workable possibility. When 1992 arrives, there may be lessening of controls, but at present you must possess a passport before you can enter France, although no visa is required for citizens of the Community. Nationals of other countries, including Australia, Canada, New Zealand, Singapore and the USA all require a visa. This can be obtained from the French Consulate General, Visa Section, 29-31, Wrights Lane, London W8. An application form is available and can be used by personal callers, who will need their passport, plus an extra passport photograph, and the relevant fee, between 09.00 and 12.30. The visa and passport will be ready for collection on the next day, between 15.00 and 16.30.

Visas can also be applied for by post, sending a stamped, self-addressed envelope of passport size for return by recorded delivery or registered post, plus the above documents and a postal order for the fee £2.20 for 3 days, £6.60 for a period of up to 3 months, and £11 for up to 3 years. Cheques cannot be accepted. You should receive your passport and visa within two or three days by this method.

British passports are obtainable from six centres in the UK, and the London Office now has the reputation of being the slowest for postal applications. Opening hours of the offices are from 09.00 to 16.30 Monday to Friday, and they are at:

Clive House, 70–78 Petty France, London SW1
India Buildings, Water Street, Liverpool 2
Olympia House, Upper Dock Street, Newport, Gwent
55 Westfield Road, Peterborough
1st Floor, Empire House, 131 West Nile Street, Glasgow
Hampton House, 47-53 High Street, Belfast

For a full passport lasting ten years, you will need to obtain an application form from one of the above offices, or from a main post office. Notes supplied with the form explain that a referee who has been acquainted with you for at least two years must witness your application. You must also produce your birth certificate, marriage certificate if you are applying in your married name, and two passport photographs. The fee is £15 or £22.50 for a joint passport. If you are a naturalised British citizen, your certificate of naturalisation must also be produced.

British Visitors' Passports which last only for a year cost £7.50 and can be supplied at any main post office if an uncancelled passport or a birth certificate together with supporting literature (pension book, etc) can be produced, you will also need two passport photographs.

You can stay in France for three months looking for a job without further formalities if you are a citizen of the EC, but after that you will need a Residence Permit – a *Carte de Séjour*. You should be able to obtain an application form from your *mairie* if you are in a rural district, or from your local Police Commissariat. In cities and large towns it is customary to go direct to the Préfecture. They will require a photo-copy of your passport together with two passport-sized photographs and, as your application is sent to Paris for processing, there will be some delay – perhaps several months. You should also produce proof of residence and a certificate from your employer, if you have already obtained a job.

The realisation that you have exactly the same rights as natives of the country when you change your residence to France does not cancel any benefits that may be due to you from the UK for at least three months after you leave. If you are entitled to UK unemployment benefit and have been claiming at a UK unemployment benefit office normally, for at least four weeks, you may continue to receive benefit for up to three months while you seek work in France, provided that you register for work as soon as possible after arrival. However, you must inform your local unemployment benefit office (UBO) of your intention to seek work in France well in advance of your departure.

If you satisfy the conditions for transfer of benefits abroad, the UBO will inform the Overseas Branch of the Department of Health and Social Security, which will send you an application form. Take this form to the equivalent of the UBO in France; leaflet UB122, obtainable from your local UBO, gives full details.

The levels of UK Social Security benefits, of course, relate to the cost of living in the UK and, depending on fluctuating exchange rates, if you live solely on these benefits, you may find it difficult to manage at first, especially as delays may occur before benefit payments recommence; therefore take enough capital with you to cover any emergency.

The Commission of the European Community publishes a series of guides entitled 'Social Security for Migrant Workers' and these may be obtained from the Department of Health and Social Security, Overseas Branch, Newcastle upon Tyne, NE98 1YX. Guide No 1 covers people going to work in France; Guide No 3 is for those sent by their employers to France, and for those normally employed in more than one state. Guide No 5 is for an employed person's family if they live in a member state other than the one in which the employed person works.

Finding Employment
When the Single European Act came into force in 1987, the long term employment picture throughout Europe took on a completely new aspect. The ultimate aim of the act was to provide an environment in which European industry could become more competitive worldwide, without setting up a Federation.

Half of the world's trade is conducted within the European Community and it is the second largest economic block in the world after North America, with a total population of around 323 million. Moreover, it has 228 of the world's top 1,000 companies (Japan has 310 and USA, 345) but where companies with profits of more than $200 million are concerned, it has 115, compared with Japan's 58, and the larger figure of 205 for the USA. Unfortunately, because the Community is made of twelve separate states, despite its many advantages it has in the past been less competitive than its largest global competitors, though its preoccupation with research and development is actually equal to that in Japan.

A look at the performance of individual countries within the European market will give some idea of the kind of balance that should be aimed for with the approach of the twenty-first century. Despite the quick rise of France in the industrial field over the past twenty-five years, at present she has far fewer of the world's top companies than Britain. Within the Community the league is something like this – Britain 112, Germany 35, France 25, Italy 17, Spain 16 and the Netherlands and Belgium 11 each. As far as the future goes, France has been ahead in planning her strategy and trying to foresee her place in the Single Market, as well as looking at the new opportunities, both for the young and for workers in all the states of the community. There can be little doubt that there will be many openings for fully trained staff at mid-management level, although a certain amount of dislocation will be encountered both before and after 1992. Those who do not recognise that this is inevitable, or who oppose the Market for fear of losing their old business without gaining anything new from the Community, have not sufficiently observed the threats that Europe is facing from the Pacific Basin. Hong Kong, Singapore, Korea and Taiwan are already preparing to follow the Japanese model for expansion in the next decade, and others, such as Thailand and Indonesia, plus China from her new port of Hong Kong, will gradually become really serious world competitors.

Having taken all these considerations into account in order to hazard a guess at possible avenues open to European expansion, those English-speaking people who now look in the direction of France can take heart from the knowledge that English, and not French, is likely to be the language of the next century. And, in having recognised this, France, whose beloved tongue was for so long the master tool of all the best intellectual exchange, has once again shown her talent for greatness. She thoroughly understands that English is already the language of science and technology, and is determined to go in that direction and make a success of it.

In line with this, during the past eighteen months, advertisements for French speaking executives sought by a wide range of international companies based in France have begun to appear in British papers and technical journals, particularly in the *Financial Times* (Wednesdays), *The Times* (Wednesdays), the *Sunday Times* and the *Independent*. Most of these advertisements are handled by management selection companies and cover every conceivable aspect of modern living. Not every advertiser requests fluent French, but all applicants clearly will be required to compete with those who can speak the language perfectly, as well as offering German and Spanish.

Those who are qualified to make the most of these opportunities should perhaps be reminded that they must be prepared to fit into an extremely dynamic background. The reasonable hours of work that only recently became commonplace for the average French worker are unlikely to apply to top flight positions where high geared conversations have a way of going on for hours. It is impossible to give detailed advice about this – each job must be thoroughly considered on its own merits, and it will be up to you to ask roundabout questions during your interview, since your prospective employer will tend to assume that you are already well acquainted with the 'conditions' appropriate to the kind of job he is offering. You may find that you are temperamentally unsuited to the kinds of demands likely to be made by French management, but a sincere desire to work hard can generally be adapted to genuine professionalism.

Entrepreneurs who make a bee-line for France sometimes do very well, but this is a style of life and money-making that cannot really be imitated by those looking around casually for an interesting, well-paid job. Above all, well-practised and fluent French is vital, plus a keen money sense. State encouragement for setting up small industries, known as PME (Petites and Moyennes Enterprises) takes various forms. Subsidies are given for job creation, and in the last few years a growing number of British craftsmen have set up small builders' and allied concerns in the provinces. Since February 1988, under EC regulations, independent manual workers (Artisans) in France must be registered with the *Chambres des Métiers*, which means that they must have acquired proper qualifications in their own countries. The same regulation applies to commercial workers, who in this case have to register with the *Chambre du Commerce*, and to workers in the hotel and catering industries who have a similar professional organisation. These provisos may make job creation far more difficult for talented amateurs, although theoretically they open the door for unlimited job creation by skilled workmen from any country in the EC.

I discussed this question with Paul and Jenny Dyer, a couple of English hoteliers who started a most successful hotel business in the Dordogne eleven years after restoring an ancient farm in a beautiful setting (Auberge du Noyer, Le Reclaud de Bouny Bas, 24260 Le Bugue). The hotel provides high quality suites of exceptional charm for those who like space and quiet in a relaxed environment. Paul Dyer felt that many people with inadequately worked out 'bright ideas', and somewhat limited capital, were tempted by the idea of good weather and wine to throw up reasonable jobs in Britain in the hope of making an easier and more pleasant life in France. We all agreed that on the whole there is far too little understanding among intending expatriates about the actual effort needed to start a business anywhere. This is particularly true in France, where the average French person is prepared to work incredibly hard at almost anything in order to make a success, and where the idea of 'office hours' is still foreign to the national character, although the working day is now shorter than it used to be.

It cannot be stressed too strongly that French people become ideal and successful bosses in small businesses because they believe that really hard work inevitably leads to success. To this end they will give up safe and well paid managerial positions to start their own firms. It follows that what you might call 'the religion of hard work' must be part and parcel of someone who is interested in becoming a self-made man in France. Since it is in the building and allied industries that some of the English have penetrated in the provinces, it is worth recording that in rural districts men arrive on site at 07.00, and even 06.30 in summer, and rarely leave again until 19.00.

Many French nationals will advise foreigners not to arrive in the country without a job, pointing to relatively recent unemployment figures when 14 per cent of the population was out of work. But others who emphasise that this figure is dropping by about 3 per cent a year, will optimistically discuss the new possibilities examined above. However, applicants who want to apply for posts advertised might be in a stronger position if they bargain from the UK.

All sorts of casual work is generally obtainable in Paris, and this has long been a classic way of learning French, though it must be stressed that recent employment difficulties have caused more nationals to look for work in fields they would not have considered previously, particularly in the tourist and catering industries. Teaching English as a foreign language comes in this category and low paid jobs are frequently advertised in the *International Herald Tribune*, as well as in the journal *Libération*. At public libraries it is also possible to read the principal journals of the trade and technical press, which carry advertisements for appropriate qualified staff. Badly paid workers of all kinds, already in full employment, also now swell the ranks of those looking for casual jobs, in order to earn 'something on the side'; there are also many unemployed immigrants who are more or less forced to *travail au noir* (do illegal work).

Anyone with technical qualifications can usefully approach the ANPE (Agence Nationale pour Emploi) offices, since theoretically all job seekers with standard training now have equal chances for any work that is going if they are from EC countries, but genuine competence in the French language is more or less essential for any work of this character, as well as for conversation of almost any kind with staff in job seeking agencies. Those without qualifications should be reminded that, as in Britain, there will be long queues of the unemployed waiting for anything that turns up.

Student Opportunities and Jobs
Finishing one's education in France or Switzerland has for more than a century been the accepted norm for language-orientated children of the financially secure. Now it is within the reach of everyone, and those who are not academically inclined can widen their life experiences, working in conservation, child care, archaeology, on farms, etc. All kinds of grants and bursaries are available for students specialising in languages.

The key to these opportunities is available at the Central Bureau, a British Government office funded by the Department of Education and Science, as well as by the Scottish Education Department and the Department of Education for Northern Ireland. Offices of the Bureau are located at Seymour House, Seymour Mews, London W1H 9PE (Tel: 01 486 5101); 3 Bruntsfield Crescent, Edinburgh EH10 4HD (Tel: 031 447 8024); 16 Malone Road, Belfast BT9 5BN (Tel: 0232 664418/9). The publications listed below, plus first rate information sheets on 'Working in France', 'Volunteer Work', 'Au Pair Posts', 'Work Camps', 'Grape Picking', 'Farm Work', 'Study Grants' and the 350-page volume *Working Holidays 1990*, giving details on work permits, visas, insurance and health requirements, and unemployment benefits, etc, (approximately £6.95, or £7.70 including first class UK postage; £11.60 air mail postage worldwide) are all available from the above addresses.

One aspect of student opportunities that seems to be very little understood is the availability of travel and subsistence grants made by local education authorities for approved study visits. While public libraries in the UK, and the libraries of the British Council Overseas can produce useful publications on the subject of financial aid, The Central Bureau's own 300-page publication

Study Holidays is the definitive document for all those thinking about language learning, or the study of language as part of wider art and literature study. This offers practical information on sources of bursaries, grants and scholarships, and lists useful publications. It also has invaluable practical information about accommodation and travel. Costing £5.50, it is available by post at £6.20 including first class UK postage, or £10.25 including airmail postage worldwide, or from any good bookshop.

Another valuable source of financial support can be tapped through the Training Commission, Dept CW 15C05, The Paddock, Frizing Hall, Bradford, BD9 4HD, whose pamphlet costs £1.60 (Tel: 0274 541391). This can often be referred to at schools or careers offices, and is specifically aimed at young people of high academic promise who desire higher education courses; they can apply for supplementary awards, or for sponsorship from employers and professional bodies.

Students planning future research into language and linguistics should obtain *Research Grants* published by the Centre for Information on Language Teaching and Research (CILT), Regent's College, Inner Circle, Regent's Park, London NW1 4NS (Tel: 01 486 8221).

Many other grants are listed by the Central Bureau's own information Sheet No 9, including Higher Education Grants through LEA (Tel: 01 934 9000 for 'Grants to Students'); 'The grants Register 87-89' covering also exchange opportunities, competitions, prizes, professional and vocational awards, and help for students in unexpected financial difficulties is published by Macmillan, Houndmills, Basingstoke, Hants RG21 2XS; 'Study Abroad XXVI 1989 - 91' lists scholarships, fellowships, assistantships, and travel grants at university level throughout the world – from Unesco, 7 Place de Fontenoy, 75700, Paris, France, and is obtainable in the UK through HMSO; 'Higher Education in the European Community' for those wishing to study in the EC is available from Official Publications of the European Communities, 5 rue du Commerce, Boite Postale 1003 2985 Luxembourg, and also obtainable from HMSO.

The Youth Exchange Centre at the address Seymour House (see p81) has now taken the place of the former Youth and Community Department, jointly sponsored by the Central Bureau and the British Council; it issues a free pamphlet introducing ideas such as 'Project Europe', travel bursaries available to students in full- or part-time education wishing to carry out a study project in a member state of the European Community. 'Home from Home' is an international guide available for £3.50 about home stays and exchange visits, etc. Some job ideas are listed below.

An interesting organisation based in London, handling private language courses available in different regions is the French Centre, of Chepstow Lodge, 61/69 Chepstow Place, London W2 4TR (Tel: 01 221 8134). These courses, of up to one month, include accommodation, a set timetable of intensive teaching, sports activities such as tennis, riding, windsurfing, and excursions in the vicinity, etc, plus evening activities. One such, for the over eighteens, is based at Montpellier University, with 4 weeks costing 7,500Fr, inclusive (about £750).

Teaching and Allied Jobs

Many temporary jobs in the teaching and allied professions can be obtained through the Central Bureau. Noteworthy is the Young Worker Exchange programme, which is sponsored by the European Commission. This enables young people to obtain vocational experience in another European Community country through work placement with a host employer, or through a programme of meetings and visits which focus on a particular industry or aspect of an occupation.

Appointments lasting a year, as Junior Language Assistants, are available for school leavers intending to study French at an institution of higher education. A teacher already fully qualified and in work can take advantage of the Teacher Exchange Scheme to exchange a permanent post with a colleague in France.

Au pair posts open to women between the ages of 18 and 30, for a minimum of six months and a maximum of eighteen months can also be investigated through the Bureau. Comprehensive details are given in the volume mentioned above, *Working Holidays*.

Actually, au pair positions are open to both sexes, but girls are generally preferred. These positions should not be confused with ordinary domestic employment as they are governed by different employment and entry regulations. Full details of these points are discussed in *Working Holidays*. Such positions, of course, are sought primarily by those who have a year to fill in before going to university, and the status sought is as a member of the family.

In return for board, lodging and pocket money, light household duties to include simple cooking and care of children up to 30 hours a week must be undertaken. Pocket money is usually £20 a week. Occasionally the host family pays either single or return fare after a stay of twelve months or more. The Central Bureau advises that agencies be used to obtain this kind of position; the present fee payable is about £46, including VAT.

Here it is necessary to sound a word of caution about the many agencies operating in France that have sprung into being as a result of the present difficult employment situation. Temporary labour is being used increasingly because in this way employers can escape trade union and legislative control. Where seasonal jobs are concerned, temporary workers can, of course, be sacked without compensation. Naturally this leads to various kinds of exploitation and it is particularly important for foreigners with less than a perfect understanding of French not to be deceived about any handy job that seems to be coming their way.

Archaeological excavation and grape picking are still two favourite temporary jobs, and work on countryside conservation can be considered as parallel to these, although the projects are of shorter term. Farmwork may be available from May until October, but French students and regular seasonal workers compete for these open air activities. All these jobs are more or less physically demanding and the heat of summer can be more trying than continuous winter rain. Accommodation in the vineyards is sometimes too primitive even to be called basic; even so the cost of food and accommodation will be deducted from gross earnings. Some agencies provide cheap one-way travel to wine picking areas, but this should be refused as work on arrival is not guaranteed. Once again, the Central Bureau's book, *Working Holidays*, can fill you in with the addresses of local French employment agencies for the principal wine regions, but these are not likely to enter into correspondence.

Students under eighteen need parental consent before being allowed to work. Those British citizens who are looking for agricultural work lasting more than six months can apply through a British Jobcentre which will forward applications to the ANPE.

Unless staying more than three months, European Community nationals do not need work permits, but residence permits will be required (see p76, *Working Formalities*). Birth certificates also must be produced before you can be affiliated to the national insurance scheme.

Family Welfare – Health and Education

(Both health and education are covered in greater detail in Part II, chapters 9 and 11).

Many British people are aware that DSS Certificate E111 is the passport to parallel health care in France (though you have to pay for something like 20 per cent of your treatment). What is not so clear is that a stay in hospital which might be the result of an accident, something covered entirely in Britain, could cost you an extra £60 a day, even if you were completely covered by E111, and you would in fact have to pay the entire hospital charge yourself and wait for a refund – £120 a day would be about the minimum.

Another little understood aspect is that despite your long standing NHS contributions etc, once you become domiciled in France you can't return home and expect free hospital treatment as if you had never left. It is particularly important, therefore, not to give up your home address and your GP if your stay in France is likely to be of limited duration.

Additional private insurance is, of course, the answer, and many companies cover a variety of needs. One of the best policies for medical emergency services, or for full cover abroad is offered by Europ Assistance, 252 High Street, Croydon, Surrey CR0 1NF, underwritten by Lloyds and Eagle Star Group. A comprehensive policy can cover the various members of your family and be for a genuine short stay or for up to a year.

Expatriates planning stays longer than a year are warned that Certificate E111 is not the one they want. Certificate E106 will cover you if you decide to work for a long period and wish to continue paying contributions in the UK; E119 provides cover for unemployed people seeking employment in France and E121 is for those on a retirement pension or widow's benefit if they have decided to reside permanently in France. Certificate E109 provides equivalent medical cover for children at boarding school in France.

You may have heard about the excellence of French Lycées, the widening of the curriculum, and the more progressive outlook since the sixties, but depending on your children's present school, you could still discover that the system in France lags behind, and that the methods of selection to ensure transfer from one stage to the next leave much to be desired, being widely criticised by middle class parents.

However, much depends on the calibre of staff in the prospective school. At the same time, it is important not to be too complacent about your children's educational future if you plan to spend several years in France, particularly if languages have never been a strong point. You would be well advised to talk to your children's own teachers, and also a special educational consultant before plunging them into the French version of education, however good that education may be for the French themselves.

Of course, if your children can begin with the Ecole Maternelle, or go to primary school at five, they will then become bilingual naturally. Nevertheless, you will still discover that British attitudes to what one might call intensive school work, and to class competitiveness, are more relaxed than those in France, and to measure up, and perhaps later to compete for the important *Grandes écoles*, your children will need to work in the way more common in our grandparents' day than in our own.

Mastering the Language

In Part II you will find useful information about this, but aspiring executives will need a more basic approach. The luxury route to acquiring an acceptable accent and the ability to express complicated ideas is through the International Centre for Study and Leisure, a non-profit making organisation based at Château Valouze in the Dordogne, 40 miles (64km) east of Bordeaux (La Roche Chalais, France; Tel: 53 91 44 28) where a new style of teaching known as the 'bilingual- binomial' method is practised. Here you are paired off with a French partner and told only to speak each other's language. But computer technology, classes, games, social evenings etc, all play their part.

One week's intensive course here costs about £730, including tuition and full board. But language training for British industry is also handled by the London Chamber of Commerce, and the Linguaphone Institute of London publishes details. Lunchtime French-speaking sessions appeal to the budget conscious (see also *Student Opportunities*, pp81–3 for the work of the French Centre in London).

4
Setting Up House

Flats and Houses
At one time most foreigners who went to work in France, particularly in Paris, assumed that they would have no difficulty in finding an apartment. Industrialisation and the drift to the towns of a large part of the rural population changed this easy situation, and although many large blocks of flats were erected from the sixties onwards, the arrival of French immigrants again aggravated the position. Luckily, the increasing decentralisation of industry, and the growing importance of 'regionalism', acted as a counter-attraction, expanding provincial towns and cities as more and more jobs were provided away from the Paris agglomeration. But the Ile-de-France still remains the most densely populated area, so although flats may be purchased in the suburbs for reasonable down payments plus monthly instalments, they are not really easier to rent.

Indeed, the desperate flat seeker who already has a good French job to go to, but nowhere to live, may well cast a longing eye at what appear to be empty tower blocks on the peripheries of various cities. In fact these flats are either owned by local councils or by large local employers, and are empty only because drastic renovation is required. They are little townships, locally known as *cités* or *HLM*s – *Habitations à Loyer Modéré*, and available only to certain classes or low-paid worker. It is difficult to understand the dereliction of a *quartier* planned as recently as the sixties, with tennis courts, swimming pool, and so on, but it all stemmed from bursts of lawlessness in the early eighties, when the local working people moved out of the blocks as soon as North African immigrants moved in. This state of affairs is being tackled by the National Committee for the Social Development of the Quartiers, which represents central government; and in a country which has long prided itself on not being racist, there are hopeful signs, such as the attitude of the Mayor of Mantes, who claims that diversity of cultures brings a richness to France and to Europe, so that 'immigrants are a plus. . .'

Maybe in 1992 EC citizens will be considered in the allocation of flats needed to produce a workable social mix in the *quartiers* which are being re-planned but, for the time being, even the genuinely needy French have to queue for accommodation in the private sector. So for younger expatriates, although flat dwelling seems to be the most pleasant and carefree way of starting out in a foreign country, joining long queues for expensive rented accommodation may not be regarded as a sensible solution. Those who have short term housing supplied by their new employers are indeed lucky. Those who do not, might think in terms of asking their employers for financial guarantees acceptable to bankers who specialise in providing mortgages for flat and house purchase. For this a certain amount of capital would be required, probably something between 20 and 30 per cent of the house selling price. There are no building societies in France (though, again, 1992 may bring changes in this field) but specialist bankers like Le Henin can provide mortgages. And because the French Government now actively encourages house purchase *Crédit Foncier, Crédit Agricole, Banque Populaire*, and so on, may finance you up to 50 per cent if you are an EC citizen, although if you are British, some banks will be much more generous than this, a new departure. (This subject is covered in Appendix B, p188, under Househunting and the Loan Position.)

Although these terms are nothing like as generous as those provided by UK building societies, it is worth bearing in mind that property prices in France are still very reasonable. Nor is it necessary to purchase apartments rather than houses on the grounds that they are all that is 'affordable'. In fact it may be prudent to examine carefully an alternative that is not available in Britain. This is the possibility of choosing a small chalet or villa from the catalogue of commercial builders who operate large-scale construction companies all over the country. Such companies will erect for you an economical, one-storey *pavillon, chartreuse, farmette,* and so on, with or without a garage, on the outskirts of the town or city where your new job will be centred, at about one third of the price for a similar thing at home. Should you need something ready to walk into, you can buy an older model of one of these houses with the construction problems remedied.

A spanking, solid, pre-war house, in an unfashionable area, could cost between £30,000 and £70,000. But choosing your own site and having something really new always has distinct charms, though in this case you must be sure of two things – that the land on offer will definitely carry with it a *Certificate d' Urbanisme* – and that the design of the house you have chosen will not conflict with local regional norms.

In fact, the *Certificate d'Urbanisme* which is issued by the local planning authority (and is part of all house sales), has inbuilt clauses concerned with what architecture may or may not be acceptable locally, and what usage, public works, etc, are applicable to the property or may be envisaged in the years to come. In this respect it covers many of the same aspects of house purchase as the 'Searches' that must be carried out under conveyancing in English Law. Your local planning authority is located at the *mairie*, the headquarters of your commune, if you are building in a rural area. In a town, your authority is the *ville*. You can safely take the advice of your builder over the formalities, but you still may not actually be given permission. If only small changes are required, it is simpler in the long run to fall in with the local authority's wishes.

It is necessary to go to the trouble of interpreting the architectural limitations for yourself, despite the fact that you may intend to buy a building that appears to be planned down to the last door knob. This is because the exact location of your new house must also be considered in connection with its artistic effect upon the local environment, and whereas your builder may be excellent, his decisions and interpretations may not always be correct. Property in or near towns or villages that are *classé* (which means that they are in the 'National Monument' classification) have to satisfy strict demands concerning styles of roof, actual tiles used, colour of paint and so on. So if the address of your proposed building links you with *classé* property that may be even several kilometres away, you may have less freedom over what you thought of as inessentials. Also, should you buy a site that has an old property on it in a *classé* town or village, there will be many restrictions on the use of materials for repair, as well as requiring faithful reproduction of parts that need renewal (similar to the regulations governing 'Listed Buildings' in the UK).

Some people will assure you that buying a commercially

designed house will let you off mistakes on the planning front but there have been various cases where the ministry responsible for the maintenance of local public monuments (churches, *châteaux* etc) has complained after the erection of typical commercial designs incorporating stereotyped balconies, ironwork, architraves, external lighting, and so on, and the unfortunate new owners have been obliged to change these at considerable expense. Where the commercial builders offer to change plans in advance to suit local conditions, it is up to you to ascertain that the alterations included in the final building do not involve you in considerable 'extras'.

You will pay your builder by instalments, probably 15 per cent when planning permission is granted, 20 per cent when footings are done, 55 per cent when walls and roof are up, and 5 per cent when fittings, electrical work, joinery, plumbing and central heating are in; but these figures will vary according to the financial status of the builder. If you do not keep up the payments agreed, he can stop work and sue you. All builders must give a *garantie décennale*, or ten-year guarantee, for faults in the structure. But baths, wcs, plumbing fixtures, etc, are guaranteed only for two years.

Should any of these questions not seem sufficiently clear to you, you should not risk buying the land – *terrain à bâtir* – where you may not actually be able to build the house of your choice, and a chat with the local *mairie* could be invaluable. If this is your first exchange in what you hope will be your own commune, you may well be impressed by the trouble that is taken, and the interest shown in you, their future neighbour. Where the *mairie* is deep in the country, you will certainly meet the *maire* himself and begin to get an entirely new and pleasant insight into paternalistic local government.

There is also a further snag about the sale of any agricultural land that has previously been part of a larger property, in that it must be offered to neighbouring *cultivateurs* before you have the option to purchase. Your *mairie* will also advise you about the government organisation – SAFER or SOGAP - which has the prior right to purchase all farmland which is put up for sale. This may cause delay.

The use of an estate agent – *agent immobilier* – to help find the kind of accommodation you would like is becoming increasingly widespread throughout France. But first-time buyers and renters rarely seem to be aware that payment of fees and deposits is essentially different from standard practice in the UK. In some respects the final outcome is less chancy, but it is very important, at the outset, to be absolutely clear about the amount of commission payable, and the amount of *frais* – expenses – that will have to be met.

Since the changing of the law in 1986, you may occasionally be able to bargain over the amount of commission you are prepared to pay as the purchaser of a property, but this must be settled in advance. Commission is normally settled at 10 per cent of properties up to 300,000 Fr in price, 8 per cent between 300,000 and 700,000 Fr, and 6 per cent above this figure. The price quoted to purchasers *includes* the agent's commission; the only extra on top of that is the *notaire* (solicitor's) fees. In the UK the seller pays the agent's commission and there is a similar custom in the Paris region. In the provinces, the commission will be split between buyer and seller according to the agreement.

In what is essentially a buyers' market at the present time, some of the reported 'expenses' amounting to as much as 20 per cent do seem unreasonably high, but TVA (VAT) is actually included in the purchase price, and for a new building this *is* high, 18.6 per cent. All *agents immobiliers* must be registered with the *préfecture* and have a compulsory insurance to protect their clients. The agreement that you reach concerning fees and time limits is laid down in a written contract known as the *mandat*.

Complete newcomers to house purchase in France will find no better method of acquainting themselves with basic requirements than to study one or two papers and magazines before putting themselves into the hands of a house agent. The monthly magazine *Locations et Ventes*, published by Editions Bertrand from 8 rue de Thorigny, 75003 Paris (Tel: 42 74 24 70) and readily obtainable on the 10th of each month, goes fully into such questions as purchase of land, new or old houses, resale, credit, and so on, and has hundreds of advertisements for properties all over the country. Further regional magazines are also published monthly (see Appendix A, p186).

Having come to terms with someone who appears to be a capable and helpful *agent*, it is still essential for you to settle quite clearly in your own minds what kinds of property really interest you, for although the houses you are shown may be much cheaper than in the UK, the taxes, full legal costs, commission, etc, can represent a considerable sum.

Lack of time and the desire to get something 'signed' and 'start the ball rolling' sometimes results in making half-hearted offers for a less than desirable property based on the idea that you can withdraw before contracts are exchanged. This will be your first expensive mistake. Immediately a bargain has been struck verbally, the *Sous-seing Privé*, or first contract, is signed and the deposit (usually 10 per cent) paid. This is equivalent, in England, to the sale contract, and should you wish to back out, the entire deposit is forfeited. At the same time, if the vendor wishes to back out, or to sell to another purchaser, he must repay double the amount of the deposit.

The first contract also includes various conditions that must be fulfilled before the sale can be ratified; one is connected with the time required to obtain a loan or the renunciation of anyone having pre-emptive rights over the land or buildings. If one of these *conditions suspensives* is not satisfied, the deposit can, in fact, be reclaimed, since neither party has any control over such a happening. The condition relating to the raising of a loan by the purchaser is more generous than a parallel situation in the UK, where the difficulty of obtaining a loan quickly often results in the complete loss of the sale.

Sometimes several people own a house that is put up for sale, eg, through inheritance, and in this case negotiations can be prolonged. If the property is particularly desirable, and minors are involved, it is necessary to ask the *Tribunal de Tutelle* (a court that looks after the inheritance of children) to sign on their behalf. However, where some of the adult owners live at a considerable distance, it may be more sensible to drop out before making an offer. Usually the *agent* is able to advise on how keen the owners are to sell, though this may not always be in his interest. Not all *agents* are equally open about handling a '*héritage*', and it is always worth asking direct questions about the vendors before you reach the stage of signing. It is also relevant here to look into the question of '*viager*' sales (see Part II, chapter 11).

Dates for completion, and the method of payment (whether in instalments or upon signing the final document) are also laid down, and if insufficient time is left for the buyer to raise the balance of the purchase price, he will be obliged to pay interest to cover his default. Although these dates, once written in, are binding, they are negotiable, and need to be very carefully thought out in advance, since they ultimately entail either bank-to-bank transfer or the pre-existence of a French bank account that can be used when needed.

Standing behind the *agent*, quite out of sight, but in fact the most important man in the sale, is the *notaire*. It is he who orchestrates the *conditions suspensives* mentioned above and who finally deposits the *Acte authentique* with the Land Registry. In many regions, where no *agent* has been instructed by the sellers, this is the man with whom you will first come into contact. As you motor through town and country, you will often see weatherbeaten For Sale notices, usually hand-written – *A Vendre* – and followed by a telephone number. If it does not connect with the family selling the property, this number often leads you straight to the *notaire*, an important man in the community known by the legal term of *maître* instead of *monsieur*, and often operating from an imposing house or suite of offices. The *notaire* is licensed by the government and carries out much the same work as an English solicitor. In fact the exact translation of his title is 'conveyancer', and conveyancing lies at the heart of his work, even though he acts for the state as a tax gatherer and land registrar, and a large proportion of his hefty fee is paid to the government.

Varying according to the size of the sale, you will have to reckon on the following fee for the *notaire*:

5.3 per cent on sales from 0 – 20,000 Fr
3.3 per cent (plus 340 Fr) on sales from 20,000 – 40,000 Fr
1.65 per cent (plus 1,000 Fr) on sales from 40,000 – 110,000 Fr
0.825 per cent (plus 1,907,50 Fr) for amounts above 110,000 Fr

VAT will be payable on this fee (18.6 per cent); registration fee varying about 4.2 per cent; *Taxe communale* at 1.2 per cent; *Taxe regionale* varying about 1.15 per cent; salary *du Conservateur des Hypothèques* at 0.1 per cent, plus the '*Coût de l'Acte*' (searches, notices, authentication, etc), brings the total to somewhere between 10 per cent and 12 per cent.

After all these complexities, young expatriates with a city job may opt to hire an apartment somehow, come what may, although credit facilities can also be obtained for purchasing a lease. Many would-be tenants prefer this course and even offer more than the asking price in order to be put at the top of the queue. This device is known as a *surenchère*. Once the sale is agreed, it goes forward in a similar mode to the purchase of a house. In Paris it is necessary to think in terms rather similar to those in London – you consult a house agent about local possibilities (having first ascertained the kind of commission payable) and you also comb the small advertisements in daily and weekly papers – *Le Figaro* is a favourite source. To be the first in the field when answering, you must have a sheaf of impeccable references handy, plus a bank account in a more than handsome state, and the knowledge that your present salary, and job, whether you have children, or pets, etc, will all come under the eagle eye of the future landlord, who in any case is bound to have a score or so of other first-class applicants for what he has to offer. With all this in mind, your attitude to living in the centre may well suffer a reverse. On the other hand, if you are fortunate enough to land a flat that is more or less acceptable, there is still the hurdle of the tenancy agreement. Frequently a quarter's rent will be demanded as a deposit (*dépôt de garantie*), and if you are obliged to pay out this kind of money, you should be aware that the *garantie* may be non-returnable in the event of any damage to the *appartement* fabric, or to its decoration and contents. Unless your knowledge of the French language is well above average, you may certainly quail at what you stand to lose. However, with a flat in a good *quartier* you can insist on, and rely on getting, a detailed, clear inventory, and you yourself should check that stains, cracks, wear, etc, are entered in full and *countersigned* before your occupation commences. This can be vital.

Even if the deposit for the flat is only one month's rent, it is important to understand that seemingly unreasonable claims for reinstatement may still have to be met. And this is more a reflection of life in capital cities than anything to do with France itself. Fortunately, flats in the provinces are easier to come by, and cheaper to rent, but the regulations governing them tend to be similar.

It is easy in preliminary discussions about the agreement to forget about insurance. Roughly, the owners of furnished apartments look after the entire insurance, but it is important to realise that your own effects will not be covered in the case of burglary.

You must also satisfy yourself about contents belonging to your landlord in case you are expected to cover these yourself against theft and damage. The extremely high price of French insurance in all fields might make it worthwhile to take out a British 'All Risks' cover before leaving the UK, but this will be very much a matter of what articles you wish to insure.

Dilapidated Houses and Châteaux
Foreigners with a keen eye for bargains were the first to turn their attention to the thousands of houses that became empty all over France when the serious drift away from the land began after the last war. At that time a few hundred pounds would buy a *maison abandonée*, far from the madding crowd, and a Paris-based organisation organised their sale.

Today you can still buy substandard ancient houses, ideal homes for retirement, at a very reasonable price. In the most sought after areas, where *résidences secondaires* are bought by Parisians as well as by foreigners, prices have at last begun to rise. That they have stayed low for so long has been connected with the fact that when M Mitterand's government came to power, many French people put their 'second homes' up for sale, fearing punitive taxation, while others ceased to regard them as a good investment. So many remained unsold that prices slumped considerably. The existence of Capital Gains Tax has also affected the picture. *L'impot sur la plus value* of 33 per cent is levied on the profit gained when you sell, which is counted as the difference between buying and selling price – inflation uplift being taken into account – but after a long period of residence, the maximum rate does not apply.

The situation at the moment is that regions cherished for their holiday homes naturally command the highest prices, but these are still way below what is charged for a similar property in the UK. Old farms, *chartreuses* (one-storey cottages), usually with a *grenier* over, terrace houses on the outskirts of towns, or more desirably situated terrace houses in southern towns, may be bought for between £12,000 and £30,000, according to condition. But on the Côte D'Azur and in the fashionable quarters of Paris, rates will be similar to those in the UK. In quoting these figures, it is also necessary to point out that similar properties in non-holiday regions may even be obtained for far less. Tiny one-room cottages in Burgundy and the Loire Valley are available for as little as £4,000, and this figure would be echoed in regions like the Landes, Haute Provence, Franche Comté, and so on, although the average 'cheap' cottage will cost something like £12,000 to £14,000, and similar properties that have already been rescued will be double that amount. In the Dordogne there is still plenty of choice, but the real bargains went long ago.

However, it must be reiterated how completely unreliable these figures are. Many houses will certainly not be habitable by normal standards, though they may have enormous possibilities; and people are shocked to find that some isolated properties, relatively recently inhabited, have no sanitation of any kind, not even the old earth closets once common in agricultural workers' dwellings in Britain. Piped water inside the house may have been laid to one sink, but more often there is no water and no well, though there is likely to be a spring somewhere quite close.

A warning must be given here about the water. Before piped water was common in rural hamlets, these *sources* provided all the drinking water of the locality, and it was the duty of the commune to have it tested periodically. You may discover that 'your' water arrives freezing cold from a great depth before it runs into a trough formerly used for laundry by the local village. Though it may indeed taste delicious, and many inhabitants will tell you that
they prefer it to the piped water, you cannot rely on it being safe to drink. In some districts the wide use of fertilisers and weedkillers sully both *sources* and streams, and the *maire* should be able to tell you where the water can be analysed. Unfortunately, this is becoming increasingly expensive and difficult. The chemical analysis is easy enough, but a biological analysis needs to be done without delay. Notwithstanding this, there are still people who regularly drink spring water, especially in limestone country. In fact, it is far cheaper and easier to have mains water laid to your relatively remote house in France than it is anywhere in England, though for a truly remote property, it is likely to be impossible. In this case, where no spring is available, an outside flat-topped concrete tank collects rainwater.

Mains electricity is also quite easy and cheap to acquire at present. At the outset you may only be provided with a limited number of kilowatts, but it is worth enquiring about the rates for offpeak electricity and the possibility of going 'all electric'.

Above Collioure on the Cote Vermeille, Rousillon, under the Alberes mountains, the natural barrier between France and Spain. Church with lighthouse tower and 11th-century castle. *(Fototour). Below* A typical 17th–18th century Dordogne barn. With golden stone walls 2 feet thick, faded tiles and massive interior timbers, it could make an impressive conversion. *(Fototour)*

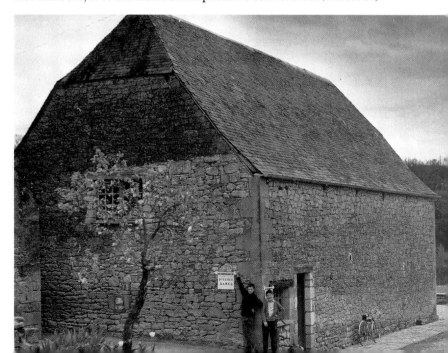

Above Typical houses and chalets of the Midi, in St Jean Pied de Pont (Pyrénées Atlantiques). Note the ornamental eaves, found throughout the Basque country. *(Fototour). Below* The sixteenth-century town of Puy l'Eveque in the Lot. *(Comité-Départmental du Lot; photo R. Nimetz)*

Above Central square of St Céré, where an opera festival takes place each July. *(Comité-Départmental du Lot). Below* Boule is played throughout the south of France, in the streets and squares rather than on special pitches. This is Nîmes, in Provence. *(Fototour)*

Overleaf The Pont Valentré at Cahors, chief town of the Lot *(Comité-Départmental du Lot)*

Above St Cirq Lapopie, towering above the valley of the River Lot. *(Comité-Départmental du Lot; photo J. de Chalain). Below* Cyclists and a flock of sheep outside the seventeenth-century château at Assier in the north eastern corner of the Lot. *(Comité-Départmental du Lot)*

Above Pig rooting for truffles. Thes pigs become pork after one season, because they learn to eat the truffles as soon as they are disinterred. *(Comité-Départmental du Lot; photo R. Delvert).* *Below* Shepherd with flock of sheep; their milk provides the raw material for Roquefort cheese. *(Comité-Départmental du Lot; photo R. Nimetz)*

Above A vineyard at St Vincent Rive d'Out, in the Lot valley. *(Comité-Départmental du Lot; photo R. Nimetz). Below* Oxbow loop of the River Lot west of Cahors. Note the symmetry of the fields. *(Comité-Départmental du Lot; photo R. Delvert)*

Throughout rural France, cooking is done by bottled gas, and some small heating stoves, as well as your hot water system, can be operated off the larger bottles or cylinders. A full-size central heating – *chauffage* – system can be run from immense tanks located outside the house. Many households find it practicable to fall back on gas, even if they prefer electricity, particularly in mountain districts and provinces like the Dordogne, where through sudden temperature changes, thunderstorms may put the electricity out of action for a few hours or a few days. Once installed, gas is much cheaper to use.

Quite apart from the provision of basic services, it will be necessary in most dilapidated houses to deal urgently with excessive damp and woodworm infestation in the roof timbers. Damp can be rectified by installing vertical damp proof courses and replastering, or by re-pointing handsome stone walls that have lost their interior plaster, plus the removal of any earth, etc, piled against the house. Depending on the kind of property, roof timbers rarely need replacing completely because of woodworm. If the roof is immense, the main beams will be very large and the sapwood only will be affected. However, the laths will probably need to be renewed. Try to get advice from a British architect known to you, or from a close friend, whose advice and knowledge of expense you can trust when discussing roof repairs. You are then in a position to consult various local builders. Alternatively you can approach the builders first if you feel able to make your own judgements about their advice; and decide in advance that you will not be hurried into an enormous programme of work 'so as to have your house in order by the next season'. Spend some weeks 'camping out' so that you can deliberate at length on what you *really* require. Obtain several estimates – *devis* – before proceeding. Some people like to consult a local architect, but in France this can be particularly expensive. Other people think in terms of a surveyor – '*un arpenteur* ', or 'expert'. An independent 'expert' can be found in the 'yellow pages'. Except for allegedly sound town houses he, too, is likely to be an extravagance. In the case of a dilapidated house, it is usually only too clear what is wrong and a local builder will be happy to talk it over with you.

At this point your dilapidated house is looking anything but a bargain, and you may wonder what you have let yourself in for. If it is set in a splendid view, with obviously good neighbours, or is of interest architecturally, you will probably cut your losses and go on, but you now know that you are likely to spend far more on reinstatement and modernisation than you actually gave for the house in the first place.

As by now you will have gained some experience, you have three choices of action: to go on and hang the expense; to look for an alternative property that is not so disastrously dilapidated, where you can camp out with a caravan while you make alterations yourself; or to change your outlook completely and go for a more expensive property that needs much less basic work.

This is where *châteaux* come into the picture. What we would regard as a large country house often earns itself the name of *château* in France. Complete with main services, and maybe a turret or two, and rich in outbuildings, if it is fairly far from the larger cities, it can cost you not so very much more than your original choice inclusive of the reclamation costs. When looking at *châteaux*, inspect something like half a dozen before making up your mind and view the outbuildings *very* thoroughly. Could you either live in these, temporarily, while the main house is made habitable, or plan to sell them, restored by yourself, when you have installed your family in the main house? In France it is common practice for householders to instruct properly qualified masons, carpenters, plumbers etc, instead of a general builder, and this piecemeal approach is ideal for the average foreigner who aims to restore a house little by little. There are now firms in Britain specialising in arranging second mortgages for expatriates, to enable them to raise enough funds to make substantial down payments abroad while they let their original home that they do not want to sell. Financially it is better business to borrow to buy a sounder property rather than using capital to purchase something 'easily affordable'.

One thing about these less popular, larger properties – when the Channel Tunnel is finally built, and the EC Single Market is fully established, their price will almost certainly shoot up. You can run these older properties to earth particularly easily in the Dordogne, where there are house agents especially useful to foreigners. One is an Englishman, Keith Wilson of Rue de Paris, Le Bugue; the other, M. Bavière, also of Rue de Paris, has an extremely wide knowledge of the country and the people.

5
Law in Action

The average person's contact with the law in any country mostly concerns questions of personal liberty and convenience. Few of us commit crimes, but in adapting to a legal system other than the one we have absorbed since youth, we may make a few innocent blunders that will inadvertently harass people we should prefer not to disturb.

Anyone seriously interested in this aspect of life abroad should certainly read *The Legal Beagle Goes to France* by Bill Thomas, a solicitor who has made his name answering legal questions on the BBC. But at the start of one's stay the following questions are probably the only ones likely to bother us.

Speeding and Parking
You must acquaint yourself with all the different categories of speed limit, but the one where you are most likely to get caught out is on single carriageway ordinary roads with a limit of 56mph (90kmph), or 50mph (80kmph) if the roads are wet. These roads are so often empty as far as the eye can see that nearly everyone is tempted to do a spot of speeding (and you may be similarly tempted in a deserted town, where the limit is 37mph/60 kmph). On the spot fines are the rule here and the range is between 1,300 to 2,500 Fr. The speed limits are endorsed by traffic police on motor bikes, in pairs, and your speed will be measured by radar. And if you find that you are always being tempted to speed on these 'safe' roads, do be warned that the one time not to do it is mid-morning on a Sunday, when the speed cops are particularly vigilant. Read up Bill Thomas on this entire subject before you make some rather expensive 'mistakes'. Incidentally, overstaying on a parking meter can be similarly pricey.

Fishing - La Pêche
Even tiny brooks in the middle of a field are protected, and your teenage children may be in trouble if they take out minuscule trout. Fishing is so well organised in France that all the

formalities must be obeyed. There is a basic licence for the local fishing club which usually can be obtained at a fishing tackle shop, or at the relevant *Syndicat d'Initiative* – local tourist office. This costs around £3 and for an extra fee you will obtain stamps, or some other appropriate authorisation entitling you to fish in a certain way (number or rods, etc) in certain waters. It is a mistake to poach, even in the smallest brook. Waters have to be stocked and looked after, and they are patrolled by water guards who will want to see your licence.

Do not be too optimistic about what you will actually catch in France. The trout you see everywhere on sale are reared in tanks. Fly fishing is unknown. In some places the local sport is to fish in specially stocked *étangs*. Quite often the fishing tackle headquarters are also bookshops, and picking the brains of the proprietor will be well received and worthwhile. But it is almost always difficult to find out in advance the true names of local fish. Sometimes you will see it on sale in a market as 'River Fish'. In the Dordogne the best local fish is simply called 'Dordogne Fish', and very good it is. In Burgundy they eat eel – *anguille*, tench – *tanche, perche,* and *carpe* (or *carpillon*). Dace are *vandoise* (you will find the average small dictionary unhelpful over fish names). Fish of the salmonidae are to be found in various foothills, and salmon themselves are found in the Pyrénées foothills.

The excellent pamphlet 'Fishing all over France', issued by the French Government Tourist Office, has been unavailable for some time, but they may be able to provide useful local pamphlets.

Living off the Land
Despite the existence of the modern Country Code (and this is well laid out in another essential book *Walking in France*, by Rob Hunter (which gives invaluable information about footpaths in all the regions), many of us were brought up on the ancient law that laid down the right to cull berries and fruits from the hedgerows. In France no such law exists and if you pick wild raspberries, blackberries, sloes, hops, mushrooms and wild cherries you may find yourself in trouble. Actually you are likely to be able to get permission quite easily to pick blackberries and wild raspberries, but walnuts, hazelnuts, mushrooms and other fruits can be a much valued 'crop'. And it is standard practice to leave

all windfalls, whether they be nuts, apples, pears, etc, wherever you find them.

In the case of verges to agricultural land you will need to find out whether the land belongs to the municipality or to a private *proprietaire* - the local *mairie* can tell you this. On mountains follow local custom. In the autumn the rural French turn out in force to gather *myrtilles* for jam or tarts on the mountain sides. These are picked off the bushes with a kind of metal comb which can be bought in ironmongers' shops. There appears to be no restriction to this harvest, but it would be prudent to avoid hillsides immediately adjacent to farms or villages.

La Chasse

This is a major event in the French sporting year and is in fact shooting, not hunting as we know it. The season opens some time in September, usually on a date settled locally, and generally involves a combination of Sundays and one weekday. This arrangement benefits the working population – *La Chasse* is by no means an exclusive form of relaxation, though it is preponderantly male. It is widely reported in the local press and can become the main topic of conversation for weeks at a time.

At other times of the year permission for shooting predators such as hawks and magpies can be obtained by *propriétaires* – landowners and farmers. These special permissions are usually given by an official supervising a large district, and the *mairie* can give you guidance about it. Theoretically, this kind of permission is not easy to obtain because the birds concerned may be preserved species, and there are abuses where financial considerations have been known to override the law.

Watching a party of sportsmen fan out across some unfortunate farmer's field sometimes demonstrates that few of them are experienced in the use of firearms, although there are supposed to be tests and extensive formalities before the *Permis de Chasse*, a hunting licence, can be issued. Every season, taking the country as a whole, there are shooting 'accidents' in which people are fatally injured, and Frenchmen are not allowed to hunt unless they have a comprehensive insurance designed to cover fatal accidents.

Visitors can obtain a temporary permit for forty-eight hours shooting twice yearly, but this will not be granted unless appropriate insurance cover already exists. This permit will cost you about 170Fr and for the *préfecture* in the district where you want to shoot you must produce two photographs. They will also want to see your passport and your shotgun licence (plus certified translation, with copy).

You cannot, of course, just walk into France with a shotgun under your arm. The *Douanes* will expect you to provide proof that you are a member of a recognised shooting club, and show your Shot Gun Certificate, and on your exit from the UK you should also show these to the British Customs Officer. Alternatively, you can take three copies of the translation of your Shot Gun Certificate, plus the original, and apply to the French authorities in advance for permission for local game shooting, when you will probably be allowed to have two shotguns and one hundred cartridges for each. Needless to say, it is an extremely serious offence to smuggle in shotguns without declaring them.

If you have already made some good local contacts by the time you finish these formalities, you will find that an interest in the *chasse* will open many doors, from the *château* down to the humblest tenant farmer, and your neighbours will explain which shooting is reserved for the local syndicate. All sorts of by-laws govern how and where you may go shooting, and what you may aim for, and here there are very definite customs that you will have to observe. Above all, as a newcomer, don't think you can go it alone, and do respect the precise regulations about keeping the proper distance from dwelling houses. Domestic animals, dogs, cats, etc, tend to get involved, disturbing marksmen and making an unfortunate end; if you have to deal with their irate owners, the law may well go against you.

The law against disturbing people on their private property also extends to photography. You may not take a photograph of any private property unless the owner consents, and very severe penalties follow the publication of photographs that were allowed but did not include a request for permission to publish.

You will find the French as a whole rather sensitive about their liberties and privacy, and you must understand that this is an offshoot of the wars that have been foisted upon them, as well as an inheritance from the days of the *ancien régime* from which they struggled so hard to be free. At the same time, the law about trespass is rather lenient, and some rather telling remarks about this are made in the book *Walking in France*, mentioned above.

Part II
LIFE DAY BY DAY

Rosalind Mazzawi

6
Learning French

Until your French is really fluent, you will be greatly helped by studying *La Politesse* – formal manners – just the appropriate address, prefixed with 'but', plus a smile, and a marked shrug of the shoulders – '*Mais, Monsieur*', '*Mais, Madame*' – can bring some temporary difficulty onto a different level. Personal contact is established.

Unfortunately, few foreigners ever use the correct form of address – it is always necessary to add '*Madame*', '*Monsieur*', when greeting or thanking someone, whoever they may be. '*Bon jour*', '*Bon soir*', '*Merci*', etc, by themselves are completely unacceptable, and unhappily give rise to a suspicion that this lack of politeness is meant to convey inferiority of the person you are speaking to.

After a few months' residence you should be able to manage the use of the proper pronouns. When are you to use '*tu*' (the equivalent of 'thou', which is no longer used in English)? In fact, except in the case of children, with whom you always use '*tu*', you must stick to the more formal '*vous*'. '*Tu*' is reserved for family members and friends of long standing, especially those from school, university, or military service; '*vous*' is for the rest of the world. A great step forward is taken in a friendship when one person requests the other to use '*tu*' instead of '*vous*'. Young people tend to be more informal and address each other as '*tu*' as soon as they meet; lovers may use '*tu*' when alone together, and '*vous*' in public, depending upon how acknowledged the relationship may be, and how formal their background. Sometimes, married couples from an aristocratic family say '*vous*' to each other in public, and '*chèr(e) ami(e)*' rather than using each other's first name.

It is usual for people to shake hands when meeting each other for the first time each day; if they are good friends, they may kiss each other on both cheeks, whether of the same or opposite sex. In Paris, particularly, this custom is carried to excess with four pecks, two on each cheek. It is extremely discourteous to refuse;

indeed, friends may be permanently lost by such a refusal. Young women, when approached by gentlemen with obviously amorous intentions, may turn their cheeks in the most literal fashion, to accept a friendly greeting.

New arrivals who do not already speak French can comfort themselves by learning a few slang expressions to help them to get by until they are able to express themselves. The words *truc* and *machin* are invaluable here; they mean, interchangeably, 'thingummy' and 'whatsit', and can be used to indicate a problem concerning a motor car, any piece of household or agricultural machinery, or the speaker's health. Thus *'Il y a un truc qui ne marche pas dans la voiture'*, or *'Je ne comprends pas ce qu'il a, ce machin'* (used of a non-functioning lawn mower), or *'J'ai un truc qui me fait très mal au ventre'* (Something is giving me a terrible stomach-ache). Beware, *la machine* means a machine, only.

These *trucs* (this word also means a trick, or knack) are for temporary or emergency use. The beginner will best learn French on the spot, by attending classes, or by having a private teacher, and by *speaking the language as much as possible with those who know no other*. There is an obvious disadvantage here in arriving with a family since English obviously will be the language of family conversation. Children are quick to pick up the language, especially if they play with local children. Older people will find French classes provided, at a modest sum, in nearly all the regional universities, as well as by private institutions.

In Paris the *Alliance Française* has an extensive programme, which can be joined every month and at any level. This organisation is the French equivalent of the British Council, and exists to promote the French language and French culture, both overseas, and in France to foreigners. Berlitz is the oldest established and the most efficient of the private language schools. The Sorbonne provides a course in French civilisation, with some language work too, but this is for students who already speak some French. *Au pair* jobs require the holder to attend classes, and she (or sometimes he) will certainly learn more French in the family, often acquiring a remarkable grasp of slang, or *argot*. Some temporary jobs for young people, such as grape picking in September/October in vineyards all over France (see p81) will provide a crash course in basic French, if there are no other English speaking workers. One vineyard owner at Rivesaltes, near Perpignan, employs four or five pickers each year, deliberately chosen to have no common language except French.

The French language is of Latin origin; over the centuries it has developed slowly into the tongue written and spoken today. In the beginning this was the spoken version of written Latin, as is attested by eighth and ninth century documents, and was divided into two varieties – *Langue d'Oc* in the south and *Langue d'Oil* to the north of a line stretching from Bordeaux to Lyon. Nowadays the division is perpetuated only by the *accent du Midi*; it is always possible to tell a southerner by the diphthongs and the emphasis on the final consonant of the word.

The *Académie Française* watches carefully over the language; this learned body was founded in 1634 by Cardinal Richelieu, to 'safeguard the language, and supervise the books published'. The forty members began to write a dictionary, the first edition of which appeared in 1694, and has been re-edited, and added to, at intervals ever since Richelieu used the services of these eminent scholars to 'ghost-write' his speeches, theological tracts, and political pamphlets; after his death the Academy became a pillar of the monarchy. Dissolved in 1793, after the Revolution, it was resuscitated by Napoleon I, who made it part of the *Institut de France*, which he founded in 1803. At this time the famous green uniform, *l'habit vert*, was designed, to be worn by the members at official ceremonies. Membership was restricted to forty and has never been changed since.

The dictionary is being constantly revised, and the Academy only allows foreign words into French after careful consideration. The living language in everyday use is to some extent ahead of the dictionary makers, as will be shown. There are, however, several other languages in France: Catalan in the south west, in the *département* of the *Pyrénées Orientales*; Provençal in Provence; Breton in Brittany; and Basque in the Pyrénées. In Alsace a patois is spoken which is basically French with a strong admixture of Low German. The French *départements* of Martinique and Guadeloupe in the Caribbean speak Creole, which is another variant of French. When universal education began in 1881, school teachers did their best to make all the children they were teaching speak French, and not use the local language or patois, so as to carry out the policy of making France 'one nation'. This worked up to a point, so that everyone educated in France had a reasonable command of the language. During the past thirty years, however, there has been a revival of local languages, in university congresses, in literature, and in the spoken word, particularly in rural areas. The central authorities have lost their fear that French will die out or be overwhelmed. There is a natural tendency to bilingualism in the human race, which can be usefully encouraged in the age of the Common Market. People who learn one language, can learn others, and frontiers will become less of a barrier. Alsace is a leader here, for there are Alsacian writers in French, in German, and in Alsacian. Some manage to be trilingual and write in all three.

English, as the modern international language, is widely understood in France, but until relatively recently people preferred not to speak it unless absolutely necessary. Now, the relentless approach of the European Community in 1992 is obliging ambitious French people to step outside their traditional attitudes. Of course, the French in England, or the English in France, are in any case obliged to try to express themselves in the other's language.

English-speaking readers will be interested to know that there is a dictionary containing some 2,500 words of English origin. Many are scientific words; some form part of what is becoming an international vocabulary, such as *hi-fi*, *O.K.*, *week-end*, *leasing*, *Fast Food*, but there remain a substantial quantity that have either kept their original English meaning in French, or where it has changed. Examples of these latter include 'slip', its most common use in French being the translation of *underpants*; whereas 'slip' in English means a petticoat, or dress lining. *Catch* and *car* are two other false friends (*faux amis*) (as these non-translations are called), whilst the verb *attendre* in French gives trouble to some. It means 'to wait', whereas 'attend' in English means to go to an event, thus 'attend a concert'. The movement is different here, and a mistake could be awkward. Some words also have gone from French to English and are now regarded as Anglicisms in the French language, such as the colour auburn, for a woman's hair. This comes from the Old French word *auborne*.

Certain words have kept their meaning but changed their spelling; this can be quite confusing. 'Because' is often used in the English sense, and sometimes spelt *bicause*.

A 'caméra' in French is a *ciné-camera*, taking moving pictures only – the other kind, for still photos, is *un appareil de photo*. The carpet is transformed into a *carpette*, and there are eleven different sub-meanings for the word 'car', none of which have much to do with a motor car – 'automobile', or *voiture* in French. Basically *car* is a motor-coach, or vehicle on the railways, such as Pullman car, or sleeping car.

Many foreign artists and writers feel that they can find inspiration in Paris. No doubt, but the English speakers may be surprised to be asked about *land art*, and the influence that *lakiste* writers had on them. Landscape painting, and the Lake Poets, will be more familiar. *Lasting* in French means everlasting in English.

Lynch law, is spelt *lunch* or *linch*. A person who does this is a *lyncheur* or *lyncheuse*, and the lynching is *lynchage*. This is not an action to undertake before the meal of lunch; this word denotes one of the most confusing of the *faux amis*. In English it is the normal midday meal. French has adopted the word, but changed its meaning. A *lunch* is a collation or buffet, usually cold, served on the occasion of a family ceremony, such as a First Communion or a wedding, or an official reception. It can take place at any time of day between 10.00 and 19.30 – after that it has to be a *diner*. Caterers (*traiteurs*) often advertise *Lunches pour cérémonies et réceptions*. *Diner* in French means dinner or to dine in English. The transatlantic word diner can best be translated by *bistro*.

It is always risky for the English to discuss food in France, or even to think of recommending English edibles to a French person. The pudding or *pouding* in French, which is one of the chief items of diet in Great Britain, is little consumed in France apart from Christmas pudding which is now popular in Paris. Other foods which have no French names, and are therefore known by their English ones, are: *arrow-root, bacon, corned beef, Bovril, Cheddar* and *Stilton* cheese, *haddock, haggis, grouse* (game birds), *Marmite, muffins, kippers, ketchup, pickles,* and *porridge*. *Cocktail, gin,* and *sandwich* have passed into the French language; so has the work *drink*; and *express*, for coffee, comes from the Italian *espresso*. Grapefruit is *pamplemousse* in French, but the English word is often used. Curry, spelt *kari*, from the Hindi, is now becoming a popular dish in Paris; Indian restaurants are springing up apace. The word 'Williams' describes a type of pear, and also the liqueur made from it. Cake in English is *gâteau* in

French, but there is also a *cake* in French which describes a Dundee type, full of preserved fruit. This is normally consumed at tea-time, or what is known in France as *le five o'clock.*

Where liquids are concerned, *Coca Cola* is universal, and most people in France know about *sherry, soda water, ale,* or *pale ale, stout,* and *Bourbon whisky. Punch* and *grog* are popular in winter under the same names. *Peppermint* is a liqueur (otherwise it is *menthe*); *brandy* is cognac – both appellations are used.

Beef steak is written *bifsteck*, rump steak, *rom* or *rum steck*, roast beef becomes *rosbif*, and the liquor rum becomes *rhum. Chips* are what potato crisps in packets are called in France. English chips are *pommes frites* on the other side of the Channel.

For the fans of *western* movies (NB: they are called Westerns in French too), it is useful to know that the Sheriff becomes a *Shérif.* A radio or TV female announcer is a *speakerine*; if you are interested in spiritualism remember that it is *spiritisme* in French; adjective, *spirite*. The spirits which are drunk are *alcools.* The squatter who takes over an empty house is a *squatter* in French too, but his squatting is *squattage.* Tackle for a lifting operation is *tacle*, and whereas tarmac is used in English, the French prefer the correct word *tarmacadam*, from the name of the inventor of this road surfacing. Tilt in English means simply to change position to another angle; *faire tilt* in French is suddenly to attract another person's attention, or to produce a sudden and striking effect. The common turnip becomes *turnep*, or *turneps* – also *navet*, a purely French word, with the subsidiary meaning of a literary or artistic work which is bad and uninteresting.

Slight wounds are painted in English-speaking countries with iodine, which is brownish in colour. In France *mercurochrome* is used for the same purpose; this is bright red. The word week-end is sometimes spelt *ouiquende*; this means that it has definitely become part of the French language.

The word, or phrase, *avoirdupois* presents a particular problem, for it is made up of three French words: *avoir du poids* (having the weight of), which have passed into English as a system of weighing all goods other than precious metals, jewels, and medicines. The present meaning, in both English and French, applies to the Anglo-Saxon countries for goods, other than the above, sold by weight, rather than item or volume.

Breeds of dogs developed in Britain have kept their English

names; thus we have 'terriers' of various kinds – Airedale, bull, fox, Scottish, and Skye terriers, beagles, cocker (spaniels), as also springers and King Charles's. Foxhounds, pointers, retrievers, and setters are other breeds common to both countries. Horse racing first took place in Newmarket in the seventeenth century, on a regular organised basis, under King Charles II, and only came to France in the nineteenth. The vocabulary is therefore almost entirely English (eg, *racer, sprinter, stayer, groom, lad, steeplechase, turf*), as it is also for *fox hunting*.

Cheviot sheep's wool is known as *Cheviotte*, and the collie dog used to herd these sheep is spelt *colley*. To continue in the animal world, a pony is a *poney* (male), the mare, or female, being known as a *ponette*. This describes the smaller sized equine, such as the Shetland or Dartmoor; when they get bigger, such as the Connemara or Halflinger breed, they become *double poneys*.

Where clothes are concerned 'boots' are ankle high only; when longer they become *bottes*. The *duffle* or *duffel* coat has the same two spellings, and the same meaning. *Pyjamas*, another Hindi word, are also worn in France, but lose their 's'. *Liberty* is the material made and sold by the shop of that name; a *panty* is an elastic panty girdle. Tights or panty-hose become *collants* in French. Sports shoes are usually known as *baskets* in French, a name derived from shoes worn to play the game of basket ball.

All chic Frenchmen yearn for British clothes, reputed to be the best in the world for men; they would be happy in a *Shetland wool pullover*, and a *blazer* with *whipcord* trousers, covered by a *trench coat*, or a *raglan tweed*. If they go to Scotland, they will immediately don a *kilt*, or a *tartan plaid*, and add *waders* with which to go salmon fishing. A velvet *smoking* can be worn in the evening. It usually takes a new arrival some time to work out that the tail coat is *frac* - from frock coat, the old-fashioned name for full evening dress, ie, white tie and tails. Morning dress is *jaquette*; the dinner jacket or tuxedo (US) is *le smoking*, or sometimes *le smocking*. The riding coat has become *redingote*. Shorts, worn in hot weather, lose their 's' to become *le short*, and are usually *much* shorter. The English type, which cover the leg almost to the knee, are usually known as *le Bermuda*. *Knickerbockers* and *knickers* are synonymous in French, and describe full tweed trousers which stop below the knee, usually worn for mountain trekking and playing golf, and often known as plus-fours in English.

Business and commerce began in Britain, and therefore the vocabulary is to a great extent English. Words common to both languages include: *automation, ballast, budget, cash and carry, cash flow, charter, discount, dumping, establishment, factoring, franchising, holding company, fixing* (for money rates), *clearing house, sponsor* and *sponsoring, stock, trust, time sharing, management, marketing*, and *merchandising.* The words describing construction equipment, and various means of transport, such as *ferry boat*, and *station wagon* (also *brake*) are English too.

This chapter has covered a fraction of the ground of joint, or opposed, vocabulary, which as pointed out can be treacherous. Newcomers will have much diversion in finding out for themselves the likenesses and differences.

7

Food and the French

Parisians are geared to meeting each other in cafés, which exist in hundreds all over the city, and then eating together in restaurants, rather than inviting their friends to dine at home. Invitations to meals at home tend either to be very casual '*à la fortune du pot*', or else extremely formal, with an elaborate five course meal, showing off the best china, glass, and silver, often with help hired for the evening in the background. This type of invitation is intended to impress, rather than please, the guest; English-type dinner parties between friends are extremely rare. However, in the country hospitality at home is more frequent, time and space being available. Sometimes Parisians will even invite foreign friends to spend a weekend at their country home (*résidence sécondaire*), although the same foreigners may never be invited to the Paris apartment. Since foreigners usually find this inconsistency puzzling, and even disquieting, it is comforting to realise that there is nothing personal in it. The practice of rarely entertaining people for meals in Paris, and of seldom inviting them home, is a deeply ingrained national habit which you might as well accept in advance. If friendly feelings do develop from contacts in the country, it could be amusing to forget that you are never 'asked back', and still go ahead with the kinds of parties you like to hold in the UK.

It seems that people actually feel more natural and less bound by convention when in a rural atmosphere. Most people own their *résidences sécondaires* but tend to be rent-paying tenants of their city apartments; this is often for tax purposes, but also betrays the desire to own a little piece of land, and make provision for retirement, even if it is impossible to live there all year round. On the other hand, many an old family house in the country, though rarely used, is maintained from generation to generation, for the devotion to the family is linked with an enduring affection for the *pays* and money doesn't come into it.

When invited to a house for the first time, it is courteous to bring cut flowers – always an odd number – a plant, or chocolates for the hostess. If invited to a celebration – birthday, First Communion, or wedding – the guest should bring or send in advance a suitable gift. As in Britain, brides often set up wedding gift lists at large stores. After a dinner or party, a note or telephone call of thanks is correct; those wishing to leave a particularly good impression may send flowers then. When invited to a meal, it is customary to arrive ten minutes late rather than early; if the guests find themselves in front of the door a little too early, a walk around the block, or a quick drink in the nearest café, is the best solution.

Cafés
Cafés have two, sometimes even three, prices for the same cup of coffee or glass of wine, according to whether it is consumed standing up at the bar, seated inside at a table, or, in fashionable parts of the city, outside on the terrace. These terraces are open to the elements in summer, and are closed with glass windows in winter. In the south of France, parasols are normally provided for each table. Pastis, an aniseed-flavoured drink which turns milky when water is added, is a refreshing and favourite summer drink. It can be alcoholic or non-alcoholic. It should be remembered that all soft drinks are normally *more* expensive than wine or beer. Beer is either draught (*pression*) or bottled, the latter costing slightly more. In the wine growing areas a glass of the local wine is the most economical drink. All international soft drinks are available; those particular to France are Gini – a type of bitter lemon, *diabolo menthe* – lemonade with peppermint syrup, and *grenadine* – pomegranate syrup with soda water. Fruit syrups diluted with plain or soda water are much enjoyed; some people find them too sweet. A tablespoon of straight lemon juice restores the balance. Fresh orange, grapefruit or lemon juices may be obtained in most cafés; ask for *orange, pamplemousse*, or *citron pressé*. Nuts, olives, and potato crisps (known as chips in French – English fried chipped potatoes are *frites*) are provided if the customer orders an expensive and fashionable drink such as whisky or a cocktail.

For the hungry, most cafés provide ham, cheese, or pâté sandwiches in long *banquettes*, or toasted cheese and ham sandwiches on square slices of milk bread. These are known as *Croque Monsieur* - a *Croque Madame* has a fried egg on top. Mixed salads are also served at lunch time. Once established in a café, one order will last for as long as you may wish to remain, although occasionally in a crowded and popular establishment the waiter may ask pointedly if *Monsieur* or *Madame* would like anything else. However, many people actually establish their headquarters in a café near their home or place of work, meet their friends or business acquaintances, and even write letters, or draft books and articles there. It is normal to leave the small change as an extra tip, although 10 to 15 per cent service charge is added to the bill automatically, unlike the USA, where it must be calculated separately by the customer.

Mealtimes and Food Shopping
Food is a serious business in France, and one of the main preoccupations of most citizens. Anyone coming to live in the country should recognise this interest, and be prepared from time to time to spend long hours at table, eating, drinking, and discussing the affairs of the world. Previous and future meals are apt to form a large part of the conversation, and small talk is often on the same subject; people exchange and compare recipes, and the names of good (and bad) restaurants. The necessity of nourishment has turned into an aesthetic pleasure, and few criticise this transformation.

The usual eating pattern is that of a light breakfast – *petit déjeuner* – croissants or fresh bread and jam, occasionally yoghurt or fruit juice, and coffee, tea, or hot chocolate. Coffee may be served with milk, as *café au lait* ; chocolate, of course, contains milk and is delectable when whipped to frothy lightness. Tea is normally made with a tea-bag, and milk is rarely added, although a slice of lemon may sometimes appear. Sugar is always provided, though the purists say that *café au lait* is better without it. There are no morning milk deliveries to the door in France (nor indeed in any country except Britain and the Irish Republic). In any event, fresh milk is not much drunk in France; *lait sterilisé*, which always tastes 'cooked', is available in grocers everywhere. In country districts one can still get unpasteurised, fresh milk from farms, often with cream on the top.

There is always a friendly baker around the corner in French cities whose fresh bread and croissants perfume the early morning air, and tempt many people to nip out and get some for breakfast.

The motto of most bakers is 'service' – often he will sell you half a loaf if he hasn't the size you want. A full list of shapes, sizes and price is usually displayed. Square sliced loaves are available in some urban supermarkets, though very rarely in the provinces. There is a growing tendency in France, as elsewhere, to eat whole foods, so that some bakers now make *pain de campagne* (country bread), *pain de seigle* (rye bread), or *pain complet* (wholemeal bread), as well as the normal long white *baguettes* or flutes. In Paris, bread can normally be sliced on a machine according to the thickness required, as long as it is not too fresh. Warm bread will not slice. Another delectable variety is a rye loaf with walnuts or raisins or onions added (*pain aux noix, aux raisins,* or *aux oignons*). A new five-grain *baguette* is now being made by a few Parisian bakers, and this always sells quickly.

Many bakers are also *pâtissiers*, though in the provinces these roles still tend to be kept apart, and the *boulangerie* will often be the one shop open, early or late, and throughout the lunch hour. A small town may have six *boulangeries* to one *pâtissier*. The *pâtisserie* dispenses various delicious cakes, individual size or larger, and it is always possible to purchase a portion of a fruit tart, or flan as it would be described in Britain, with the fruit on top and the pastry underneath. The two are linked by a cream and egg custard, and the fruit is often topped by an apricot glaze. The quality naturally varies, but such flans are rarely too sweet, even if they do add some calories. There are infinite varieties of chocolate, coffee, chestnut, and fruit-flavoured *pâtisseries*, sometimes decorated with fruit peel, nuts, angelica, or sugar sequins. Also, there are drier macaroons and *palmiers* (pigs' ears). Sweet biscuits are known as *biscuits*, and the dry, salty ones, again available in enormous variety, are *biscottes*.

Normally lunch, or *déjeuner*, is the most important meal of the day, or at least the most leisurely. Offices and factories have a one and a half to two hour lunch break (rarely less) providing excellent (and subsidised) meals in canteens, or by means of luncheon vouchers. (Again, in the provinces, this break is almost always two hours.) Four courses are the rule; an entrée, which may be mixed raw vegetables, or a slice of pâté, or egg mayonnaise, or steamed leeks in a French dressing – or something more elaborate such as a cheese soufflé, avocado with shrimps, or smoked salmon for a celebration. Then there is a meat or fish course with one or two vegetables, followed by a choice of cheese, always served with bread, not biscuits, and butter only with certain cheeses such as Gorgonzola. Dessert, with cakes as described above, or else plain fruit, ends the meal, and coffee is served thereafter. People often have apéritifs, port, vermouth, or Ricard, before the meal, and drink red or white wine with it. Scotch whisky, neat or with a little ice, is a fashionable apéritif in some circles; liqueurs and brandy are more often drunk in the evening after a formal dinner, where the menu will be much the same as that of the lunch described above, but probably with a fish course or a 'special' omelette – eg, with truffles, – and the vegetables served with the main meat or game dish, and a salad before the cheese. In some private houses vegetables are served separately from the meat; this is an old-fashioned habit that is now dying out. The idea is to enable the diner to appreciate the different flavours separately. Restaurants no longer do this unless specifically requested, in order to economise on time and waiters' labours.

The evening meal, dinner, is often lighter than at noon and may consist of soup, a cheese or egg dish, or a simple casserole, followed by fruit. In France, there are few class distinctions to do with eating, but one of these is that larger dinners of the traditional four courses will be eaten higher up the social scale – although there are obvious regional dishes, such as *choucroute* (spiced cabbage with ham and sausages) in Alsace, mussels and oysters in Brittany, *cassoulet* in Toulouse, *bouillabaisse* and stuffed vegetables in the south of France, goose, chestnut, and walnut dishes in the Dordogne, and so on. But everyone eats *andouillettes* (chitterlings), fried onions, or *boudin noir* (black pudding, served with apples) if they like them – the rich, the poor, and the in-between. Lunch is normally at 12 noon; indeed, in the provinces few people are seen in the streets between 12 and 2pm (civil servants may go to luncheon at 11.45) and only a few food shops stay open after midday, generally closing at 12.30. Often an apéritif hour precedes dinner which may be served at any time after 7.30pm. Here the only economic division seems to be that the less prosperous drink their apéritif in the local bistro, and the better-off in their own homes. Unless they are going to an entertainment, theatre, cinema, or lecture, people do not generally go to cafés after dinner; the British custom of an evening spent drinking in a pub has no equivalent in France. Of course, when the cinemas come out, particularly in Paris, people often go to a café for a nightcap.

Tea drinking is becoming more popular, and so are shops specialising in a myriad different brands of tea and coffee. When families visit each other, either tea or coffee may be served, but without anything to eat. Tea as a meal is a rarity, except for ladies who play bridge, or who wish to visit each other in the afternoon. Sometimes charitable tea parties take place in rarefied circles. Children, when they come home from school, get a *casse croûte* of bread and chocolate, or a sandwich, to stave off the pangs of hunger until supper time. Secondary schools often keep the children to do two hours of homework after classes end, so they do not leave until 6pm, and as they advance up the educational ladder, they have even more homework to get through.

Most offices, businesses, and factories have at least one annual banquet, when management and employees put on their best clothes to attend what is usually a jolly and friendly occasion. The custom of the office Christmas party is creeping in, but food is always served along with the drink. Cocktail parties with a few biscuits and crisps only are considered very inferior; it is customary to provide an endless supply of tiny open sandwiches, hot sausages on sticks, and mushroom and shrimp vol-au-vents. Both private hostesses and companies who offered only biscuits or crisps would soon lose custom, although *en famille*, and between close friends, the newly introduced ranges of cocktail biscuits are acceptable.

All this food and drink is purchased from various sources, chiefly from the wholesale or local market. The Paris wholesale market is at Rungis, on the southern fringe of the city on the way to Orly Airport. Meat, fish, cheese, fruit, vegetables, and flowers are sold in wholesale, or large retail, quantities to purchasers from local markets, shops, restaurants, and private houses, who appear from 04.00 until about 08.00, all transactions being an occasion for discussion, comparison, and expertise.

Throughout the country there are open-air street markets, two or three days a week, and also covered markets. In Paris, for instance, the markets in the rue de Buci near St Germain des Près, is open every day from 08.00 to 13.00, and again from 16.00 to 20.00, except on Sunday afternoons and Mondays. The same is true of the Marché de l'Aligre, near the Bastille; here, however, there are two markets, a covered one which sells choicer and more expensive food, and one consisting of stalls in the street with fruit and vegetables of vast choice and quantity, at rock bottom prices. The variety and elegant arrangement of meat and vegetables is amazing, as is the interest displayed by most stall holders in the quality of their merchandise and the satisfaction of the customers. Except at the very busiest times, they are glad to chat and to explain where the best watercress or cherries come from. The cheese purveyor will sell ripe cheese to be eaten at once, or some that needs maturing for consumption a few days later as the customer wishes.

Again, in Levallois, just outside the Paris ring road, *la Périphérique* , there is a market three days a week, on Tuesdays, Fridays, and Sundays, which has the usual fruit and vegetables, fish and meat – which has sections for sellers of horse-meat, other butchers' meat, and poultry and game, including rabbit, a very popular item in France. Guinea fowl are also common; *la pintade* is considered a cut above chicken for a lunch party. Turkey legs, breasts, and wings, sold in separate pieces, have also entered the French market. Ducks are often available; a goose must be ordered in advance. Then there is a *charcuterie* stall, selling pâté, cooked meat, and salami of many kinds, and a cheese merchant who presents his wares in impeccable condition, and can always advise on the best. He also supplies butter and eggs. Two suppliers, one of whom is Portuguese, have dried beans, pulses, and rice; the Portuguese also has sardines in oil, olive oil, hot sauces, and dried cod fish (*bacalão*). Bread, cakes and croissants of cut-price quality are purveyed at cut-price rates (the local baker is better), and there are the usual stalls for kitchen utensils, cheap clothes and shoes, jewellery, watches, and cosmetics. Books at reduced prices are next door to a vendor of flowers and small pot plants. A haberdasher selling buttons, elastic, needles and thread is usually there; occasional traders include sellers of porcelain, photo frames, and initialled writing paper. On Sundays, some enterprising Arab boys sell bunches of fresh parsley, coriander and mint at 1.50Fr each. They do a thriving trade.

Most of these items are to be found in markets all over France. Vegetable and flower plants, garden and other equipment, as well as clothing, are to be found in country markets, with the addition in some places of regional specialities, or Chinese and Vietnamese cooked food. Most people buy fresh food in their local market. However, there has been considerable growth in the number of super- and hyper-markets, both in the cities and on their outskirts, where shopping malls in the American style are to be found. These are suitable for car-borne citizens, and carry a vast variety of goods; all types of alcoholic and non-alcoholic drinks, non-perishable groceries, household goods, gardening equipment, etc. The best known, throughout France, are Auchan, Mammouth, Carrefour, Euromarché, and Leclerc. Most are open until 22.00, and also sell petrol 10 to 15 per cent cheaper. The Leclerc chain is well known for its low prices and the aggressive policy of its owner, Edouard Leclerc, in taking on the petrol firms, and also the undertakers, a tightly closed shop.

One little-known fact, and of great convenience, is that butchers in France will generally cook meat purchased from them at little extra cost, if they have the facilities. Many possess a *rôtisserie*, or revolving spit, at the entrance to their shop on which they broil chickens to be sold ready-to-eat; others have ovens. The purchaser of a leg of lamb or joint of beef or of pork which costs 100Fr may have it roasted on the spit or in the oven for 10Fr more, if this is requested at the time of purchase.

Naturally, people eat in restaurants as well as at home. Restaurants of all kinds flourish, from *le fast food* hamburger joint to the local *bistro*, to a Michelin three-star gastronomic temple. Almost everyone has a favourite neighbourhood restaurant where they are known, and where the *patron* (or more often the *patronne*), remembers that Henri likes his pepper steak well done, and that Madeleine prefers rice with her calves' liver. There is not such exaggerated wine expertise as there is in Britain. In fact, few French people seem to study wine at all, and at home will drink table wines delivered in a 5l plastic carboy and working out at not more than about 6Fr a litre. Those who want something a little better choose the local wine, or a table wine costing no more than 12Fr a bottle, with a good Bordeaux for special occasions. As France is a wine producing country, foreign wines are always scarce and dearer. You will rarely find Hungarian 'Bull's Blood' in Toulouse, or a German 'Steinwein' in Rennes. Alsatian wines, however, compare very favourably with German hock.

One fear of the French wine growers is that, with the admission of Spain and Portugal to the European Common Market, a flood of their cheap wine will make it uneconomic to produce table wine in France, as production costs are higher. This problem has not yet been solved, but probably an elaborate system of subsidies and quotas, as has already taken place with milk, will be set up. In Languedoc/Roussillon, *vin ordinaire* at present costs 5Fr a litre, and is perfectly drinkable.

It is rare to see people drunk in public; this is quite unacceptable socially. Some drink steadily for years, and die eventually of cirrhosis of the liver, but they rarely appear to be affected. Those who drink no wine at all are even rarer, though there are a good many who do not consume hard liquor.

In country districts, however, it is the custom to offer – and to consume – when visiting a neighbour, small glasses of the local *marc* (grape alcohol), fruit liqueur, or even Pastis. This is especially true of the *gendarmerie* on routine visits, and anyone beginning a long stay should remember that it is advisable to cement friendly relationships with the forces of the law.

Good cognac is drunk amongst connoisseurs; champagne is a celebration drink for everyone, but is drunk more and more by 'successful' people everywhere on quite ordinary occasions. A recent survey showed that over 90 per cent of the population of France has tasted champagne on one or more occasion. Sparkling wine, such as Vouvray from the Saumur district, or Blanquette de Limoux from the town of that name in Roussillon, in south west France, is almost as good as some champagne. The name 'champagne' is restricted by law to the sparkling wine produced in the area around Reims and Epernay. Do not let a champagne manufacturer hear you praise sparkling wine from anywhere else.

Cognac is grape alcohol, distilled and very carefully blended, and comes from the towns of Cognac and Jarnac in the Charente. It is exported all over the world, but particularly to south east Asia, where the Chinese drink it like wine. Highest sales in the world are in Hong Kong, followed by Singapore and Malaysia. Executives of the cognac firms who visit the Far East have to have strong heads, for they are expected to keep up with their hosts at the many official, and less official, lunches and dinners to which they are invited. The result in France is that both the champagne and the cognac-producing regions are very prosperous, and this shows in the well ordered landscape, and the well tended houses and villages. There are also some excellent restaurants. Here the importance of eating is matched by the importance of producing the best possible drink to accompany the food.

8
Work and Play

Working hours in France are planned around a lunch break of two hours; they are, normally, 08.00 to 12.00, and then 14/14.30 to 18.00, and sometimes later. Executives often remain in their offices until 19.00; senior civil servants may work until 21.00 but take a lunch break until 15.00.

Travel

It is rarer than in Britain for employees who work in the centre of a great city, such as Paris, to live miles away in the more distant suburbs, although there are some who travel for as much as an hour each way to work. Public transport is cheap, convenient, and frequent; the French grumble about it, but they do not realise how fortunate they are.

There is a Métro station within five minutes' walk of almost every street in Paris; the buses run regularly, although they can be blocked in traffic jams despite the special bus lanes, and the RER (*Reseau Express Régionale*) provides fast access to the city centre from a long way off – St Germain en Laye and St Rémy les Chevreuse, to name two termini. Of course, the reverse of this medal is that rural areas near an RER station have become more desirable, and therefore more expensive to live in, and are rapidly becoming built up.

Travel is paid for by individual tickets, *carnets*, or booklets of ten weekly *cartes jaunes* (weekly passes), or *cartes oranges* (monthly passes), which permit unlimited travel on bus, Métro, or RER in the zones from which they are valid, and within the specified time limits. The cards are, in theory, non-transferable; a photograph of the holder must be affixed to the card when it is first purchased; it is rarely checked, although the possibility cannot be entirely ruled out. There is also a *carte intégrale*, valid for a year, like a British season ticket. Persons who invest in this might save a little money if they use it daily every month of the year, but since five weeks' holiday are now compulsory, the RATP (*Régie*

Autonome des Transports Parisiens – urban transport board) is the only beneficiary.

In the provinces the same holds good; Lyon and Marseille and Lille all have excellent Métro systems, and the bus and local rail services in such cities as Bordeaux, Grenoble, Lille, Perpignan, and Toulouse are perfectly adequate. Though coaches can be hired privately, there are no regular long-distance internal coach services because the railways (SNCF, known to irreverent English speakers as SNIFF) have the monopoly of routes; it is, nevertheless, possible to travel between England and France, or France/Spain/Italy/Greece/Morocco, etc, by coach, cheaply and comfortably by day, but with much less comfort if an overnight journey is involved. SNCF provides one of the best railway services in the world; when not on strike (as it was in December/January 1986/87, ruining Christmas travel for many), the fast trains are comfortable and punctual. The TGV (*Train Grande Vitesse* – High Speed Train) provides unrivalled speeds between Paris and Lyon (2 hours), Paris and Geneva (3 hours 30 minutes), Paris and Lausanne and Paris and Berne (both 3 hours 40 minutes), as well as other points to Marseille and Montpellier. In the summer of 1987 the TGV reached Nice, and the latest line – TGV Atlantique – is already in operation to Rennes and Nantes, and will reach Bordeaux in 1990.

The TGV has two classes, first and second; although when the TGV first began operating, the advertising made a great point of the fares being the same as those of other trains, they are often *à supplement*, with 10 to 15 per cent being added at peak times on popular routes. Thus, of the four daily services to Lausanne, two charge the normal fare, and two the extra. Seats must be reserved, and a charge of 8Fr is made for this. Reservations can be made by telephone and collected with the ticket, or made in person up to 10 minutes before departure time, if any seats are left. These seats are rather cramped for tall people in second class, but quite adequate in the more expensive first class.

There are a good many overnight trains from Paris to the Mediterranean coast and other European countries; these provide sleeping accommodation in the form of couchettes, which provide four berths in a first class compartment, six in a second class, and charge 75Fr above the normal fare for this. Also available are proper sleeping compartments for one or two persons (*wagon-lits* or T2). International trains are known as TEE (*Trans-Europ-Express*), and are quite luxurious. They also charge a supplement on normal fares.

On certain trains, including the TGVs, meals are served at the seats in first class, and can be reserved in advance. Other trains have restaurant cars, 'buffet bars' for snacks and drinks, or at least a refreshment trolley which is wheeled through the train to provide excellent hot coffee served in fragile plastic goblets, soft drinks, beer, and wine in cans, and sandwiches. All cost about one third more than in a café. The frequent traveller is well advised to take his own food on a journey, and purchase a drink as needed.

For motorists, France is covered with a network of autoroutes, or toll highways. The tolls, known as *péages*, can add as much as one third to the cost of a journey between, say, Paris and Lyon, or Paris and Toulouse. For those who travel often, it is possible to obtain a book of vouchers, pre-paid. The principle is that the autoroutes are constructed by private companies, in which the State is a shareholder of no more than 40 per cent, and must recover the construction and maintenance costs by charging users. They are certainly well maintained, and if ever there is an accident or breakdown, help arrives almost immediately. There are telephones on orange posts to summon aid, at every 1,640ft (500m) on all autoroutes.

However, long-distance automobile travel is only cheaper than the train when there are three or more persons in the car. In the cities, a car is difficult to park and easily stolen; in the country, it is more or less essential. There are big shopping malls with adequate parking on the outskirts of all the larger cities, where everything necessary for life in a consumer society may be purchased.

Despite the drop in oil prices, petrol is still expensive, well over 5Fr per litre for Super at the time of writing. The high cost of automobile travel may be offset by taking passengers who contribute towards fuel costs on a regular or occasional 'Car Pool' basis. It is rash, although sometimes charitable, to pick up hitch-hikers on the road. Young people often get about in this way, and so far the hitch-hikers run more risk than those who pick them up. Hitch-hiking, because of all sorts of crimes, is discouraged by the authorities. It is known in French as *autostop*, abbreviated to *stop*; reliable passengers can be found by contacting an organisation called *Allo Stop* (Tel: Paris 42 46 00 66), which puts car owners and prospective travellers in touch with each other. The travellers pay, basically, 16Fr per 100km. The car owner should ascertain before setting off that his insurance policy covers all car passengers, or else make them sign a waiver. The daily newspaper *Liberation* also has advertisements from people wishing to travel, or who are willing to take travellers to specific destinations.

The possession of an automobile has become totally self-defeating in the cities. What was originally intended as a comfortable means of personal transport has now become a nightmare, with no place to park, streets rendered impassable when a truck in unloading because of the serried ranks of parked cars, and endless thefts and vandalism. Dogs also damage cars, encouraged by their owners to use the wheels of parked cars as public conveniences. Indeed, the problem of dogs in cities, particularly in Paris, has become almost insoluble. They are invaluable companions for the lonely, disturbed and old, but the state of the streets in the residential areas show that there are no arrangements for canine hygiene. In Paris, the Municipality puts up rather despairing notices, '*Apprenez-lui le caniveau*' (Teach him to use the gutter), with a picture of a dog at the end of a lead in the correct position. Uniformed operatives drive green motorcycles equipped with special brushes for cleaning the pavements. Dogs, even on leads, are forbidden in most parks.

Taxis in France are ordinary motorcars, with a fare meter and light on top of the roof. This light is on when the taxi is free for hire, and switched off when the vehicle is engaged. The driver covers it with a neat black leather cover when he is off duty. Fares are comparable to those in Britain, except that each case or package in the boot is charged extra, and a taxi picked up at a station may legally add 4.50Fr to the basic fare. Only three passengers may be taken, usually on the back seat, though sometimes an obliging driver will fit one person in front. This is in direct contrast to the custom in Holland and Germany, where one person taking a cab is normally expected to sit in front beside the driver; since there is no partition in such taxis, there is no privacy either. In France, taxi drivers are often women; they tend to have dogs on the front seat, large and fierce, or small and furry, and notices requesting passengers not to smoke in *this* taxi. Taxi drivers frequently refuse to take passengers at the end of their shift (limited by law to 8 hours) unless they are going in their homeward direction; I once

133

got a cheap cab ride to Charles de Gaulle airport from the Gare du Lyon, from a homeward bound driver who lived in that direction.

At the principal railway stations, near the taxi rank, there may sometimes be seen large cars marked *'Voiture de Place'*. These are in fact chauffeur-driven cars for hire – but beware: the minimum fare is 100Fr. It is quite difficult to call for taxis by telephone; ranks and cab companies frequently do not reply. A few have a priority system whereby, by paying a modest annual subscription of about 50Fr, a client is given a special telephone number, and can call a cab which usually appears at once. He then pays the normal fare, plus a tip of 10 to 15 per cent, and will receive good service.

Air travel within France is the monopoly of Air Inter, the internal branch of Air France; a few small feeder airlines have begun to appear, but as yet they are statistically negligible. Air Inter has recently announced its intention to provide charter (cheaper) services, within France, no doubt to cope with the competition. Air France, the national State-owned airline, is notorious for always seeking to provide services at the highest possible cost; some services are excellent, some less so. International pressure, and the persistence of a travel company called 'Nouvelles Frontières', have led Air France to start what it calls *'Vols Vacances'* at lower cost to places like Guadeloupe, Martinique, and La Réunion, with passengers packed like sardines into Boeing 747s, and provided with box lunches at take off. Since Air France has a cabotage monopoly of flights to French territories, little can be done about this.

However, business travellers find it convenient to be able to go to Nice, Perpignan, or Bordeaux for the day via Air Inter. Private flying is also possible, both at main airports and smaller airstrips, and there are plenty of opportunities to learn to fly, glide, parachute, or hang glide, at specialised instruction centres throughout the country.

Travel of all kinds requires ticket purchase; these are available at all the main railway stations in Paris for train journeys beginning from any of them. But to validate it the passenger must have the date of travel punched on the ticket in a small orange machine known as a *composteur*. Travel by air or ship can be arranged through the respective travel company offices, or by means of a travel agency. These are numerous, dealing with both holiday and business travel. By shopping around it is possible to find the best terms for the journey you wish to make. 'Nouvelles Frontières' has a good selection of 'flight only' destinations, particularly to the US. But the return date must be fixed before departure, and adhered to; this can sometimes be a major drawback.

Holidays

Eleven days a year are public holidays in France, as follows:

January 1, New Year's Day

Easter Monday

May 1, Labour Day - when no work of any kind is done by anyone, except by public transport

May 8, Armistice, 1945 - end of war in Europe

Ascension Day - always on a Thursday

Whit Monday

July 14, French National Day - commemorating the capture of the Bastille in 1789

August 15, Feast of the Assumption of Our Lady

November 1, All Saints Day

November 11, Armistice Day, 1918

December 25, Christmas Day

Neither Good Friday nor Boxing Day are holidays in France. If a holiday falls on a Saturday or a Sunday, it is *not* transferred to a weekday, and extra time off is not given. For example, November 1, 1987, fell on a Sunday.

Five weeks of paid holiday are now compulsory for all employees, to be taken in two or more sections. Depending on their jobs, people take three or four weeks in July or August, and a week in February, and/or a week over Christmas/New Year. It also depends on the school holidays for those who have children. The school holidays are normally:

10 days in February - *vacances de Février*

10 days at Easter - *vacances de Paques*

12 weeks 15 June to 15 September - *grandes vacances*

1 week overlapping 1 November - *vacances de Toussaint*

10 days at Christmas - *vacances de Noël*

The dates of these holidays vary slightly in the different regions of France, the country being divided into 24 *Académies*, whose boundaries correspond roughly to those of the regions, with a few extra subdivisions. The different dates are set in order to avoid a fearful rush throughout the country at the same time. Many children go to the mountains in February and Easter holidays, either in organised school parties or with their families, and the resorts, too, prefer to spread out their customers. Since many people are great weekenders, when public holidays fall on a Tuesday or a Thursday, the intermediate weekday is often taken off as well, being deducted from the statutory five weeks. This is known as a *pont* (bridge).

Paris and its suburbs are almost deserted by the inhabitants in August; parking meters are free, and foreign tongues predominate in the streets. Many offices and businesses close down altogether, and even buying bread or a newspaper can be somewhat hazardous. The same, of course, is true of many coastal resorts between November and March, both on the Mediterranean and Atlantic coasts. On the whole, the French are urban dwellers; life in the country is for farmers, animal breeders, and a few eccentrics. There are still some splendid *châteaux* in private hands, but most of their owners will spend at least half their time in Paris or one of the larger cities.

Younger people tend to go quite far afield for their holidays; the weighty catalogue of the Nouvelles Frontières travel agency gives 102 destinations, from Austria to Sri Lanka to Yemen, and the Club Med has about half that number. Tahiti in the South Pacific is a popular destination; as it is a French overseas territory, there is no language problem, and visitors from the mother country are encouraged. The specially adventurous go to Thailand, South America, or . . . Outer Mongolia.

On the whole the French are good travellers because only those who are curious, intelligent and lively will go on strenuous journeys to far-off places. They tend, however, to be worse linguists than even the British, and if any of them know English, or the language of the country, they will do their best to conceal it. Those more set in their ways stick to France, either by having a house in a remoter country region like the Ardèche, or a seaside holiday flat, or, more modestly, returning to the same hotel or camping site each year. This gives young children some continuity, and induces familiar and friendly boredom in the adults. There are also many families who return to grandparents' farms or *résidences secondaires* in the country. Activity holidays of various kinds are becoming ever more popular, as the charms of toasting on a beach begin to pall.

Sport and Entertainment

All kinds of sport are widely practised, but apart from ski-ing, which can involve the removal of whole schools to the Alps, plus the teachers, so that lessons are not interrupted, there is not the same insistence upon them as there is in Britain. They are regarded more as spare time activities, although their importance is growing. Water sports and ski-ing, both downhill and cross country, are those indulged in by the largest number of people. Tennis, until recently the preserve of the *bourgeoisie*, is now played everywhere. Football, while much enjoyed as a spectator sport, is not an active game for many beyond the early 20s. Rugby, on the other hand, is very popular in south west France, from Toulouse to the Mediterranean coast, and a mutual passion often forms a bond between English and French on the eve of an important match. Golf is expensive and exclusive, practised largely in private clubs, but is now attracting a rapidly growing following. Cricket is not known in France. Sport for the middle aged is practised almost exclusively by the upper class.

French bowls – *pétanque* – are played throughout the country, more especially in the south, the Midi, probably because this is an outdoor sport and the weather is more suitable there.

Horse sports are practised, and watched, by a sizable minority; show jumping has been well established for years, and three-day events are gradually becoming more popular. However, by far the largest number of riders are those who go on *randonnées équestres* (horse treks) at week-ends and during their holidays. This is known as *l'équitation verte*, and provides an excellent method of getting to know the countryside. Various establishments, some excellent, some less so, organise these treks and rent out horses. Once a year there is a huge gathering of horse trekkers from all over France, in one of the smaller provincial towns, which finds this an excellent method of advertising itself.

It is less common for French than for UK riders to have their own horses, or keep them at home – there is hardly room in a city apartment! When a person does possess a horse, the animal is most often kept at livery at the local riding school (*Club Hippique*). There is not the preponderance of females involved with horses that there is in Britain; hunting (*chasse à courre*) exists but is rather different because deer – both red and roe – are the quarry, in the woods, rather than the fox in open country. Cross country riding and jumping are not so frequently associated with stag hunting.

Shooting (*la chasse*) is very popular, and eight different monthly magazines are devoted to this sport. Animals and birds hunted include wild boar, deer, pheasant, partridge, snipe, duck, pigeon, hare and rabbit; all game (*gibier*) can be seen on sale at butchers' shops in the season. Fishing (*la pêche*) in both rivers and lakes is popular, and is considered to be a peaceful, pastoral pursuit, practised on the river bank or from a dinghy. Fly fishing, as for salmon in Scotland, is rare, though adepts use the trout streams in the Alps and the Pyrénées. Worms are a more usual bait.

Mountaineering (*Alpinisme*) on both rock and ice have their enthusiasts, and some notable home-trained champions. Serious walking, using the long distance footpaths, has a growing number of adherents. There are many archers, and international archery contests take place in Paris. National teams exist for hockey, ice hockey, net-, hand-, and basket-ball. Ice skating and gymnastics are very popular TV spectacles, though it is difficult to discover how many participants are French.

The more static games, particularly chess, Scrabble, and bridge, are much enjoyed; open air chess games often take place in the parks in Paris, and draw many onlookers. Several magazines and newspapers devote columns to these three pastimes, and a panel game derived from Scrabble and instantaneous calculation is shown every evening on the television at 19.00 – *Les Chiffres et les Lettres*. The many stamp and postcard collectors have their own exhibitions, clubs, and market places.

You will see that those who come to France for a long time will have no shortage of outdoor or sporting activities. Friendly locals are usually glad to introduce new arrivals to the local club or society, and provided that the customs of the country are respected, there should be little trouble in fitting in.

As in other countries, more and more outdoor entertainment centres around television, and programme timing is predictable; on two programmes out of the three there is news at 20.00 for half an hour, and then a film which may last anything from 90 minutes to 2½ hours. In the afternoons there are programmes about animals and for children – then game-shows until the news. On Friday evenings *Apostrophes* is shown; this is a highly successful book review programme, with Bernard Pivot as compère. He is now one of the most familiar faces in France. Each week he chooses a theme: political biographies, books on animals, on polar exploration, or the Philippines, etc, and selects six or seven authors on the subject to come and talk about their approach. Pivot is an excellent host who does his homework by reading all the books discussed thoroughly beforehand; there are no awkward silences and often fascinating revelations.

Another well known TV commentator is Michel Polak, whose *Droit de Réponse* (The Right to Reply) examines various injustices in the body politic, and enables those who have suffered to put their side before the public. Some cutting social criticism results. Then there is the *Ciné-Club*, late on Friday evenings, which shows classic films, usually in series of directors or stars. The inevitable *Dallas* and *Dynasty* are popular in France, as elsewhere, and there are some good documentaries and variety programmes. The three channels, TF1, A2 and FR3, are still State owned and controlled, although TF1 is now being sold to the private sector. Advertising keeps all three more or less solvent, though until now the State has helped. *Canal +*, the fourth channel, is cable TV; anyone wishing to receive it must pay a monthly subscription. As in Britain, at least a superficial knowledge of TV programmes is necessary in order to be able to converse with neighbours, colleagues at work, and people one may meet socially.

But those who live in Paris have the lion's share of every kind of entertainment, and three weekly magazines provide information about them. These are *L'Officiel des Spectacles, Pariscope*, and *7 Jours à Paris*. Here *Pariscope* has been used, striking a happy balance, to enumerate the diversions of the capital. The cinema is probably the most popular; on average 300 different films a week can be seen somewhere in the city, often in tiny, uncomfortable cinemas somewhere in the Latin Quarter, but sometimes in luxurious establishments on the Champs Elysées. All cinema prices are reduced by about ⅓ on Mondays, and some for performances starting before 12 noon on weekdays. Students and senior citizens get weekday reductions of roughly the same amount. Paris is one of the few cities in the western world where cinemas have actually increased in number. Some 233 theatres

are listed, to include those in the nearer suburbs such as Nan-
terre – Théâtre des Amandiers – café theatres, cabarets, revues,
and other spectacles. The café theatres are not night clubs in the
British sense; rather they are sub-theatres where experimental
or slightly sexy shows may be watched whilst eating and drinking. Hard sex shows are *Spectacles Erotiques*: persons under the
age of 19 are not admitted. Eleven are listed in *Pariscope*. Under
the heading *Rencontres Liberées* are forty-three advertisements.
A similar type of entertainment is advertised in the *International
Herald Tribune*, under the heading 'Escorts and Guides', and the
left wing intellectual weekly, *Le Nouvel Observateur* ; one might
say that porn is made to pay for philosophy in this context.

Music includes classical concerts, jazz, pop, rock, and folk, as
well as classical ballet and modern dance spectacles.

For fitness fanatics, fencing, stretch, aerobics, gymnastics,
physical culture, muscular development, judo, karate, aikido,
yoga, and various types of dance are available at many gymnasia
and dance centres around the city. Swimming pools, jacuzzis,
saunas, Turkish baths and sunbeds are also popular; there are
also six ice skating and two roller skating rinks. Many of these
establishments have reduced student rates at certain times.

France has a Book Fair (*Salon du livre*) in Paris each spring,
and one in Brive la Gaillarde, in the Corrèze in the centre of
France each autumn. Both manifestations attract much public
and media interest. The French see themselves as a nation of book
lovers because the lycée literary classes place great emphasis on
reading at least fifty books a year with a broad interest in history,
art, anthropology, etc. However, the average house has not even
one bookshelf, and the British spend twice as much on books than
the French, while their public libraries lend as many as twelve
times more books than are borrowed in France. (The British claim,
apparently rightfully, that reading is their preferred leisure activity.) Actually, the French library system has improved a lot in the
last decade, and the semi-private *Bibliothèques pour Tous* has a
growing readership. Publishing has also developed a popular side
that appears to have been borrowed from the UK. In particular,
there has been much plagiarism in the field of magazine and pe-
riodical publishing of all kinds, with every imaginable hobby and
interest covered.

Most people read at least one daily paper. The chief national dailies are *Le Monde*, highly intellectual but also having a readership of 17 per cent among small merchants, shopkeepers and clerks. It is particularly well informed on foreign affairs, and somewhat left of centre. Then there is *Le Figaro*, which used to be lively and moderately right wing; it has now become tedious, and almost Fascist in its approach to such matters as immigrants and the French role in the world. *Libération* is informative and iconoclastic, and *France Soir* is the nearest thing to a tabloid that exists in France. *Le Parisien Libéré* and *Le Quotidien de Paris* are the two local Paris papers, the first being left- and the second right-wing orientated. However, the paper with the largest circulation in France is a provincial daily, *Ouest France*, which is published in Rennes and has twelve editions covering Brittany and most of Normandy. *L'Indépendant*, of Perpignan, founded in 1830, is the oldest provincial paper. Other papers of significance are *Le Haut Marne Libéré*, *La Charente Libre*, and *Le Dauphiné Libéré*. *L'Equipe* is the most evenly distributed sporting paper.

There are four weekly news magazines; *L'Express*, owned by Sir James Goldsmith, is very slick, informative, and improving regularly. Much of its advertising is for middle rank executives and high powered salesmen. *Le Point* is usually the best informed about Government policy and happenings overseas; *Le Nouvel Observateur* is the most intellectual and literary. *L'Evènement de Jeudi* is new and lively.

Wicked tongues declare that journalists of *Le Nouvel Observateur* read the news in *Le Point*, and the following week produce elaborate intellectual theories founded loosely on the facts they have gleaned from their rival. A weekly which has a wide general readership is *La Vie du Rail*, which, as well as providing admirably written information about French railways, and those in other countries, also contains the TV programmes, and general cultural and household articles. It is a bargain at 7Fr per week.

Generally, the attitude of 'I couldn't care less' is unknown in France. People do care, passionately, about all aspects of life. Some take great pride in their work and are anxious to show it off; others hate it, and do not hesitate to let all about them know it. The foreigner may find that the locals disagree with his habits and appearance, but will rarely regard him with indifference. On both sides, quite a few may be inclined to say, 'Vive la différence!'

9

Health and Social Security

This chapter is not intended to provide a complete survey of the health and social security services in France; but it outlines the main provisions, and the dealings that a foreigner may expect to have with these services and those people who administer them.

Health is the first concern; the system works quite differently from that in the UK. Any employed person, or one who has been employed for 120 hours during the previous month, is entitled to recover a certain proportion of medical expenses. These are: 75 per cent for visits to doctors and dentists who are part of the system (*conventionnés*), and 70 per cent for medicines in general. A few, essential for certain diseases, and extremely expensive, are reimbursed in full; others, not considered essential, are reimbursed at 4 per cent only; 65 per cent of auxiliary treatment, such as laboratory examinations, X-rays, and physiotherapy, is paid; 80 per cent of hospital costs is paid normally, except for specified surgical operations, when there is a complete refund (*prise en charge*); 70 per cent of transport to the hospital, by ambulance or taxi is paid. Normally the insured person must pay a hospital room fee of 25Fr per day, unless exempted on account of low income or an accident at work. If approved, a cure at a spa may obtain a 70 per cent reimbursement, to include hydrotherapy and medical expenses, plus a *per diem* payment, a second class railway ticket, and hotel expenses, for those with incomes below a certain limit.

Non-salaried persons, ie, independent workers and members of the professions, must take out a personal insurance policy through their social security office – they pay 11.5 per cent of their total income – or through their professional organisation. For health, they may insure themselves via an organisation called the RAM (*Réunion des Assureurs Maladie* – United Health Insurers).

First-time visitors from the UK are often very impressed by the health routines available in France, especially in the provinces, where the doctor appears less hard pressed than his colleagues in

142

the health service at home. But, in fact, the average French GP has a harder time than his British counterpart. His training has been much more difficult to acquire and his ultimate qualification as a doctor is by no means guaranteed. But he probably profits by a system that exacts payment at the time of consultation, a method that can materially reduce the number of time-wasting *malades imaginaires* (though to earn a decent living he still must see four patients an hour).

For all that, the French doctor often envies British GPs their permanent list of patients (he also must continually call to mind that less is spent on hospitals in France than in any other comparable country). And he must rationalise somehow the number of times he is called out at night – something that would be unthinkable in the British National Health Service. In short, the French doctor must be an idealist of high calibre to be a doctor at all, though in this form he may well have disappeared before long. At present the patient may consult whom he likes and even go to specialists, and the State will still reimburse most of the fees.

The treatment itself will vary between prescriptions of the most modern drugs, the practice of homeopathy and modified herbalism. You will have to get used to having temperatures taken rectally, and to the frequent prescription and administration of medicines as suppositories. Since most healing substances are absorbed into the body via the lower intestine, this seems sensible, but Anglo-Saxons are reputed to be squeamish about this.

It is worth recording that all large pharmacies dealing with allopathic prescriptions also stock a complete range of homeopathic remedies, something that would be frowned on in the UK. In France, homeopathy is 'orthodox' if practised by qualified doctors, but 'fringe medicine' abounds and is widely consulted – *radiesthésists*, chiropractors, hypnotists, herbalists, masseurs, faith healers – all have their following.

Reimbursement is obtained in a somewhat complicated fashion; the person needing medical attention having visited the doctor, or been visited at home, pays the fee in full. The same is done when purchasing medicines at the *pharmacie* (chemist's shop). The doctor will provide a *feuille de soins* (certificate of treatment) on which he will note the fee. Any medicines prescribed and purchased will have detachable *vignettes* (adhesive labels) on their containers; these are also affixed to the *feuille*, and the complete document is then taken, or sent, to the local social security medical office. The same applies to all the extras mentioned above. The address of this office will always be found in the local *mairie* (town hall). Reimbursement normally takes place within 15 days, directly to the insured person's bank or Post Office account. Some social security offices make direct cash payments, but this is becoming less and less common because of the risk of holding large sums of cash.

The visitor from the UK for a temporary stay will normally obtain an E111 form from his local Social Security office before setting out for France. Other countries have different arrangements; usually a personal insurance policy can be extended to cover foreign travel for a limited period. The E111 enables its holder to obtain health benefits during a visit to a member state of the EC. Should medical attention be needed, the person will act in the same fashion as the French insured citizen, giving an address for repayment either in France or at home. Outside France, payments by international money order may take up to two months to reach their destination. The person employed in France will automatically be registered for social security by the employer, and receive the same benefits as a French citizen. Actually there is a wider range of 'E' forms covering different classes of foreigners - see details in Part I, chapter 3.

Large companies often have a *mutuelle*, or private insurance scheme, which makes up the proportion not paid by the State system, and takes care of such needs as spectacles and false teeth, which are hardly reimbursed at all. Employees pay a monthly premium, which is deducted from their salaries. It is equally possible to subscribe privately to a *mutuelle*, and pay premiums on a monthly or quarterly basis.

We come next to other forms of social security benefits; those concerning family welfare - health and education - were discussed in chapter 4, but we must now consider unemployment (*chômage*) and old age pensions (*retraite vieillesse*). For salaried employees, deductions are made from the pay slips in the proportion of:

5.6 per cent for health insurances
5.7 per cent for old age pensions
1.72 per cent for unemployment benefit
1.84 per cent for extra pension fund (*retraite complémentaire*).

This last may vary from one employer to another.

These deductions are made at source. Income and local taxes are levied separately; income taxes after an annual declaration of income, and local taxes assessed upon the rent paid or the value of the dwelling occupied by its owner.

Persons are entitled to unemployment pay if they are salaried employees who:

– have been dismissed by their employer
– have been laid off for economic reasons (*licenciement économique*)
– have come to the end of a fixed term of employment
– have resigned for a legitimate reason

on condition that they have worked for at least 3 months continuously beforehand. The organisation administering unemployment payment is called ASSEDIC. Payments are made for varying lengths of time, as indicated in the table below.

Minimum length of employment	Age of person	Time for which payments are made	Possible extension
3 months during the past 12 months	All ages	3 months*	No extension
6 months during the past 12 months	Less than 50 50 and over	8 months 9 months	2 months 6 months
1 year during the past 2 years	Less than 50 50 and over	1 year, 2 months 1 year, 6 months	5 months 1 year 6 months
More than 2 years during the past 3	Between 50 and 55 55 and over	1 year, 9 months 2 years, 3 months	1 year 1 year 6 months

*In this particular case, the basic allowance cannot be granted again until 2 years have elapsed.

The amount paid varies according to the length of time worked;

it is between a minimum of 107.61Fr per day, and a maximum of 75 per cent of the last salary earned. Once the normal unemployment rights have been exhausted, the *allocation de fin de droits* (termination allowances) replaces them, for a period of up to 1 year 6 months, with a possible extension for another 9 months. The daily amount is at present (1990) 75Fr per day. The amount is reassessed twice a year, in April and October, so will be slightly more by the time that this is published. Finally, after all else is exhausted, there is the *allocation de solidarité* (solidarity allowance), which is at present 75Fr per day, renewable every six months. The conditions for obtaining it are that the person should have no more than 3,870Fr per month (to include their own personal resources and the allowance itself), should be actively seeking employment (unless they are 55 or older), and should have worked as a salaried employee for more than 5 years during the preceding 10 years.

Other allowances are paid to young people who have never worked because no jobs are available, or who take part in community enhancement projects (Travaux d'Utilité Collective). The conditions and details of all these allowances, and those eligible to receive them, are immensely complicated, but, generally speaking, any person who lives and is employed in France must pay the same contributions, and is entitled to the same benefits, as a French citizen.

Independent workers and professional persons must pay contributions as indicated in the third paragraph of this chapter, but their unemployment pay depends on the private or union arrangements that they have been able to make.

The same applies to old age pensions, although all citizens are entitled to them. They are normally paid at the age of retirement; this begins at the age of 60 for women and 65 for men, although it may be later, and, in exceptional cases, earlier. Since April 1, 1983, the basic State pension is 50 per cent of the average annual salary of the ten years when it was highest. The pensioner must be at least 60 years of age and have contributed during 37½ years in the system, in order to obtain this amount. If he has contributed for a shorter period, the pension will be reduced proportionately. The company pension can only be applied for after having requested that of the State; again, the amount will depend upon that of the contributions paid in.

Agricultural workers and farmers, miners, and railway workers (*cheminots de la SNCF*) all have special social insurance schemes, which need not concern us here. Any foreigner making a long stay in France and having a professional connection with any of them will be informed of his insurance rights and duties when he joins.

Where personal contacts with social security employees are concerned, it should be remembered that many are intelligent and cultivated people obliged to deal all day long with the lowest common denominator of human nature. This is enough to sour the most even tempered. Add to this mixture a lost soul with an imperfect command of the language, and a bad case of sunburn, or possibly eczema, and you understand why the employees are sometimes a little surly. On a good day, however, you may find someone able and willing to explain the system, who is anxious to practise his basic English and take the trouble to ensure that the foreigner is well treated and thus gains a favourable impression of French social security.

10
Your Money

Banks and the Post Office
While the banks in Britain have been quietly pulling out of their paternal role (despite their willingness to lend large sums of money to young people), French banks have been openly trying to improve their image, with large advertisements in the provincial press extolling their own virtues and the service they render to clients. Some French people meet these statements with understandable reserve, for in certain cases the affairs of a particular bank will depend too much upon the calibre of the manager, and this is something that cannot change overnight. The trend towards better service needs to be implemented rather more wholeheartedly before all clients are satisfied. Some particularly dislike the lack of secrecy about their deposits, since public undertakings such as local authorities can apply directly to a bank when residents fail to pay their bills. Actually, this system, which is a form of direct debit, can be very useful to customers who consistently keep in credit.

This means you must deal with banks that already have a good reputation, and here understanding the history of French banking will be helpful.

Many banks are members of the *Association Française des Banques*; the banking sector is directed by the Ministry of Economy and Finance and ruled by the Bank of France. There are also other types of official credit institutions; the *Crédit Agricole* and the *Caisse d'Epargne* (indicated by the sign of the *Ecureil*, or Squirrel) are those most easily dealt with by foreign residents.

To illustrate the dilemma faced by the public, over the years the *Association* has produced some rather puzzling figures: its 1984 brochure listed 506 members, of which 41 were nationalised, 55 private, 153 foreign banks and 257 other institutions. A description of the French banking system, also published by the *Association*, in its second edition updated to March 1985, stated that on 1 January 1985, the *Association* contained 362 establishments, of which 39 were nationalised, 55 private, and 148 private banks under foreign control. The other 130 establishments are undefined.

There are several reasons for the unsatisfactory relation between the banks and the general public. Most were founded in the nineteenth century, either by wealthy entrepreneurs, or by persons who persuaded others, in a time of financial and economic expansion, to invest their money in 'get-rich-quick' schemes, much like the USA in the 1920s. The novels of Emile Zola explain this atmosphere very well, particularly *La Curée*.

At the end of World War II, the larger banks were nationalised by General de Gaulle in an attempt to provide better public service. These were the *Crédit Lyonnais*, the *Société Générale*, the BNCI (*Banque Nationale pur le Commerce et l'Industrie*), and the CNEP (*Comptoir Nationale d'Escompte*). These two last-named merged in 1966 to form the BNP (*Banque Nationale de Paris*). Other banks flourished under joint stock or private ownership until 1981, when, with the advent of a socialist government, the 36 banks that held more than one billion francs deposits were nationalised. These included Worms, Rothschilds, the CCF (*Crédit Commercial de France*), *Crédit du Nord*, Paribas, Indosuez, etc. This move was generally unpopular in financial circles, and certainly did not improve efficiency.

De-nationalisation of the banks began in 1987, after Jacques Chirac became Prime Minister in the right wing victory in the 1986 election. *Paribas* was the first bank on the list; the shares put on public sale were greatly over-subscribed, so that not everyone who wanted to purchase shares was able to obtain them. The next bank on the de-nationalisation list was the *Société Générale*.

At the end of 1986, the banks declared that they were going to charge a fee for processing cheques; this proposal created such a furore among customers and consumer associations that it was withdrawn before coming into force. Various measures were proposed to make the system unworkable, including the perfectly legal one of writing a cheque on the back of a live cow. For once the insensitivity of banks to customers' needs was defeated. Many cheques, however, are written for trifling sums, and a moratorium might well be placed on cheques written for less than 100Fr (about £10).

The *Banque Populaire* (Popular Bank) is not a member of

the French banking association, nor is the *Crédit Agricole*, often described as the largest landholder in France. The *Banque Populaire*'s function is to help craftsmen and small businesses, besides handling the affairs of salaried employees in much the same fashion as other banks. The *Crédit Agricole* (National Agricultural Credit Fund) is intended to assist farmers, landowners and persons who live from choice in rural areas, and is backed by a board of administrators composed of prominent local citizens. This means that if branch staff are slow or inefficient, redress, or at least protest, is always possible. For this reason, it is preferable to bank with the *Crédit Agricole*, or another regional bank outside the capital.

The *Caisse d'Epargne* (Saving Funds Office) is an institution with a special status. It began as a popular savings bank for small deposits on which it paid a small interest. This aspect still exists, but as *l'Ecureil* (The Squirrel – from its logo) now has considerable assets, it is able to use them mostly for the benefit of its employees, who enter at the beginning of their working lives, and are expected to make their careers therein. They have a minimum of 6 weeks' holiday per year, are paid 13th and 14th month salaries, and can obtain goods and foreign travel at lower prices than those charged to the general public. Payment for a 13th, and subsequent months is a common means of providing a bonus in France; since taxes are paid upon assessment once a year, the 13th month takes care of them for many people. Otherwise tax payments must be saved out of earned or unearned income, which may necessitate a financial advisor.

L'Ecureil will lend money for house purchase by means of an *Epargne/Logement* account, as will most major banks and some specialist ones. The *Epargne/Logement* (House Savings Fund) provides credit to correspond with the money saved for house purchase, usually in the proportion of 1:3, ie, a person saving 20,000Fr can then borrow 60,000Fr more from the institution to which he has entrusted his savings. Depending upon his circumstances, and where he lives, the sum needed can be made up by a PAP, or *Prêt d'Accession à la Propriété* (loan for property ownership). A PAP is much easier to obtain in the country, preferably in a region where the local authorities are trying to prevent the drift away from the land and into the towns. Here the *Crédit Agricole* can be very helpful; any expatriate making a long stay in France in the countryside, or in a small town, would find their services useful.

However, for those obliged to live in or near Paris and with an existing account at one of the Big Four British banks – National Westminster, Lloyds, Barclays, and the Midland – the advice is to retain it. A word of warning is necessary here; these banks charge a fee to French citizens, or to foreigners who have not previously been their customers elsewhere. This is done deliberately to discourage those who would otherwise prefer them to French banks, because of their superior efficiency, or even for sheer snobbism – the National Westminster, for example, is elegantly situated in the Place Vendôme. However, British customers are accepted on British terms. The same is true of American banks: Chase Manhattan, Chemical Bank and Citibank.

The Post Office is an alternative, often preferable, to a bank for a private customer. This provides nearly all the necessary services for which banks exist: the transfer of money, the payment of bills, and the provision of savings accounts. Moreover, post offices are open for longer hours and there are more of them. Hours in the cities are 08.00 to 19.00, and 08.00 to 12.00 and 14.00 to 17.00 in country post offices; 08.00 to 12.00 each Saturday morning. A tax-free savings account of up to 65,000Fr may be held, on which interest of 6 per cent is paid (*Liveret A*), and a second account for the same amount may be held (*Liveret B*), which is taxable. It is also possible to have a checking account at the Post Office (*CCP*), and savings plans for house purchase and retirement are available. Money transfers both within France and overseas can be sent and received, often by telegraph, although this service does not exist, for some inexplicable reason, between France and the UK. Giro transfers normally get there. Nevertheless, bank-to-bank telex transfers take at least three working days, and French banks take obvious pleasure in replying negatively to telephone enquiries. A mail transfer is more satisfactory; it costs less, and the person to whom it is addressed normally receives written confirmation at the same time as the bank.

Credit cards are international, and obviously useful. Here again, the annual charge is higher from a French bank than from an English one. In France, it is a criminal offence to issue an insufficiently funded cheque, although nowadays a two-week grace period is given in which the cheque can be re-presented and paid. Overdrafts, known as *découverts*, must be arranged in advance, and are very expensive if they run over a month. However, salaried employees may normally anticipate up to one third of their salaries by arrangement.

One awkward regulation is that cheques cannot be endorsed to a third person; they can only be paid through the bank account of the person to whom they are made out. This applies to crossed cheques, and all cheques are normally crossed unless the account holder specifically requests uncrossed ones (*cheques barrés/non-barrés*). Any person requesting uncrossed cheques is automatically placed on a special list of clients to be supervised with care, both by bank and the tax office. As this supervision is well known, few people request uncrossed cheques; the very fact of demanding them indicates that they have illegal or tax-evading activities in mind. A way around the problem of endorsing cheques is to put no name upon a signed and dated cheque, and fill in the sum of money involved. This type of cheque should be handed over in person or sent by registered mail; otherwise it can be too easily diverted.

In December, 1987, an article in the *International Herald Tribune* confirmed the inconveniences of banking in France under the headline 'In France, Don't Bank on Trouble-Free Checking'. It explained that clients with non-resident accounts cannot normally have overdrafts, and foreigners must hold non-resident accounts for their first two years of residence in France. An executive of the *Association Française des Banques*, specifically responsible for promoting goodwill for the banks and finding new customers, admitted that some bank employees often do not explain the rules adequately to foreign clients, even though they are now much more lenient than they were in early 1986.

Holders of non-resident accounts can now borrow money from their bank to purchase a house or a car; they can deposit cheques up to 10,000Fr each, as well as their pay cheques. Previously, so as to control any export of French capital through these non-resident accounts, pay cheques were the only French deposits allowed. However, although there is more flexibility, it remains illegal for the banks to allow overdrafts on non-resident accounts. An executive at the Morgan Guaranty Trust in Paris said: 'If you bounce a cheque on a non-resident account, then you might not be able to have a checking account in France for whatever period the bank decides upon'.

Other alternatives are Eurocheque; the bank of the client's home country provides him with guaranteed cheques for specific amounts, and he may normally cash up to the equivalent of £200 per time in any bank in any country adhering to the scheme. This includes all the EEC countries and certain Far Eastern ones. The American Express allows green card holders to obtain $1,000 every three weeks, and gold card holders $2,000 every 3 weeks.

Postcheque is another cheque-cashing service offered by several European (non-French) banks which allows card-holders to cash cheques through the Post Office.

You need to know about the system of registering letters in France; there is a two-tier arrangement, as well as a graduated payment according to the compensation value of the package. Ordinary registered letters must be signed for normally by the person to whom they are addressed, and proof of identity shown. This is particularly true in the cities; if the addressee is absent when delivery is made, a notice is left, and the letter must be collected from the local post office. Then there are registered letters with receipt (*Avis de Réception*); this is a pink official postcard attached to the letter, which the recipient must sign. It is then returned to the sender, who is thus informed that the letter has reached its destination. This system is used for all legal documents, and between all private citizens when proof is required of despatch, and receipt, of documents.

On the other hand, automobile tax certificates, known as *Vignettes*, are not obtained from post offices but from tobacconists, usually kiosks within a café, easily recognised by a sign in red outside: *TABAC*. Fiscal stamps are also obtained here; these are required to legalise a document, and the price varies between 30 and 120Fr per stamp, according to its size – you will need the advice of a *notaire* as to what is required. This is of course another way in which the government can tax the citizen, but the advantages very often outweigh the disadvantages.

Post offices are always official establishments, and rarely, if ever, form part of general stores, as in Britain. In country districts they may take individual messages, and occasionally will sell stationery, but all have now been made as thief-proof as possible, with 1in (3cm) of bullet-proof glass between the clerk and the client. They usually carry a fair amount of cash, which is delivered by armed employees in armoured yellow Post Office vans. On occasions thieves have injured or even killed employees of the post office; proper protection for them has now been extended nationwide. It is another proof of their essential role in the community.

Insurance

Four types of insurance are normally compulsory in France: for cars, and dwellings, and against school risks and Acts of God that cause material destruction. To provide cover for this wide variety of risks, 500 insurance companies and mutual benefit organisations employ 210,000 persons, and in 1985 they did 230.9 billion Fr worth of business, with 120 million contracts taken out or renewed.

The largest companies are: GAN, or *Groupement d'Assurances Nationales* (National Insurance Group); UAP, *Union des Assurances de Paris* (Paris Insurance Union); AGF, *Assurances Générales de France* (General Insurance Company of France), and *Les Mutuelles du Mans* (Le Mans Mutual Insurance Company). These are all nationalised, and thus depend upon the State which, in agreement with the employees, appoints the chief administrators. This means that dividends do not have to be paid, and only 2 per cent of revenue is needed for administrative expenses. In theory, the surplus can be applied to the reduction of premiums, but it is unclear whether this is done. De-nationalisation of these companies is planned.

There are also many other smaller insurance companies, some specialising in particular types of risk, and others dealing with people in specific professions or occupations, such as teachers, doctors, or farmers (*La Mutualité Agricole*). Foreign insurance enterprises are also active in the French market, for example DKV and Nordstern from Germany, Generali from Italy, Groupe Bâloise and Winterthur from Switzerland, Commercial Union, General Accident, Norwich Union, Royal Exchange Insurance, and Legal & General from Britain, and AIG (American International Group) from the USA). Acronyms are much favoured in France, and can be infuriating.

In Paris it is customary to look on unknown insurance brokers with some suspicion, although in the provinces any double dealing would soon become known. You would be advised to take recommendation from trusted friends or clients, who have had satisfactory dealings for years with the same company or broker. An EC citizen owning property in France can take out insurance under written by Lloyds, with a premium payable in Sterling and claims settled in Sterling, against all household risks, and personal and public liability. The insurers say that water damage is responsible for the largest amount of claims; burst pipes and floods are common in unoccupied properties.

Two types of housing insurance are required; the first for house construction. Unless the constructor himself or his immediate family are to inhabit it, anyone building a house must insure it against faulty construction before beginning work. He would, indeed, find it difficult to sell if the insurance policy had never been taken out. Then, persons renting a house or apartment must insure it against damage to the structure, or to that of adjoining neighbours.

Where ordinary household cover is concerned, persons insuring their dwelling must give an accurate description of the premises. In some cases the larger assurance companies, such as UAP, measure the building accurately to satisfy themselves that in the event of a claim for rebuilding after a fire they will be liable only to reinstate the same sized premises. The insurance company must also be informed of any new circumstances that may increase the risk, such as the storage of inflammable materials on, or adjoining, the property. This must be sent by registered letter within eight days of knowing of the increased risk. The company then has the right to choose whether to increase the premium or to cancel the contract. Normal premiums must be paid within ten days of the date on which they are due; if not paid within a month, the policy is suspended. Insurance contracts are normally renewed once a year, and also may be cancelled at that time.

House or comprehensive car polices normally include cover against Acts of God (floods, tidal waves and earthquakes, etc). If the house is to be left uninhabited for any length of time, premiums to include theft and burglary of contents can be prohibitive. Unfortunately, as in the United Kingdom, burglary has increased greatly in recent years and a new hazard has been introduced by gangs of crooks who enter houses and flats to photograph the furniture, which they then offer for sale to likely dealers. This means that anyone finding their property has been disturbed but not robbed, should be warned to expect another visit. When there is theft or burglary, claims against the policies normally must be made within 24 hours. Claims for Acts of God can only be agreed after their status has been declared by a ministerial decree published in the *Official Journal*. For a hail damaged property, a declaration must be made within 4 days, death of farm animals within 24 hours, and crop or produce losses in up to 30 days. Accidents must normally be reported within 5 days.

It cannot be too strongly emphasised that all insurance policies should be read with the greatest care by the prospective client. Questions must be asked about anything that is not clearly understood.

A family insurance policy will often cover a schoolchild against third party, but separate insurance is desirable to protect the parents against claims for involuntary damage and accidents to other children. Personal accident cover for children within the family is also desirable, though not compulsory.

The minimum insurance cover required for automobiles is third party; depending upon where one lives, it would be wise to add theft, fire, and damage to this, with a 1,000Fr waiver (*franchise* in French). The premium will decrease if the car is kept in a garage, and this will also prevent the vehicle from ageing too quickly. Another solution, for anyone with some knowledge of car mechanics, is to buy a beat-up old banger with a reasonably good, or well repaired engine, and change it every year. Car ownership in Paris or any other large city in France is often an unnecessary luxury, but each person has different priorities.

In the country, car ownership is almost essential; insurance is usually cheaper, and garages often go with houses. Nor is the possession of a newer or smarter vehicle such a temptation to thieves. Again, it depends on use; if long distances are covered at night, it is obviously better to have a powerful and reliable means of transport.

If an accident does take place, the drivers of all cars involved fill in a form relating the circumstances, and experts from the different insurance companies involved will estimate the damage from these declarations – on site if the accident is serious. It should be remembered that if the driver and front seat passengers were not wearing seat belts, the insurance company may refuse to compensate personal injury. This point should be checked when signing the policy. Damage responsibility is apportioned according to the expert's report; less than 30 per cent liability does not usually result in the loss of a no-claim bonus.

There is a scale of prices for used cars known as '*L'Argus*', which depends on the year, the type, the model, the mileage, and the condition. A magazine of the same name appears each week with lists of cars for sale, and of prices, revised every six months. It is normal to bargain within 10 per cent either way against the Argus listing, if one is interested in purchasing any of the cars listed; it is always wise to have them examined by an expert before purchase. The insurance premium paid on a used vehicle depends on its Argus rating, rather than the actual price paid.

Some insurance companies have the unpleasant habit of considering a client who has let a car policy lapse for more than two years (perhaps because he has not owned a car during that interval) as a new client, therefore refusing to give him a no-claim discount. New drivers under 25 normally have to pay much higher insurance rates; most young people therefore arrange to drive vehicles registered in the names of their elders. A new arrival in France may also be treated as a new driver; the solution here is to have the previous insurance company, in the UK or elsewhere, provide an attestation concerning previous policies and driving record. This will be put into French by an official translator and accepted by the company whom he chooses – Prima is a suitable one – as equivalent to the same number of years in France.

Car policies which run for longer than a year are inadvisable; it is now forbidden by law for companies to cancel car policies after an accident except where the driver has been found to be under the influence of alcohol, or his licence has, on account of this accident, been withdrawn for more than one month.

Policy holders may cancel their contracts before term if the premium is increased, the risk diminished, or an insured object is lost or stolen. Death, house moving, divorce, a change of profession, or retirement, are also valid reasons for cancellation.

Foreigners arriving in France for a long stay will doubtless retain their original life and retirement policies, but may be interested in extra cover. There are various types of life insurance available. The simplest consists in paying a sum of money to a beneficiary after the death of the person contracting the insurance. This may be limited to a particular period, as for example on a hazardous journey, or a more conventional type, after death – which is bound to occur eventually. Premiums are obviously higher in the second eventuality. Delayed capital payment means that premiums are paid for a given period of time, and a capital sum is then made available to the subscriber at a time agreed upon, if he is still alive. If he has already died, the insurance company keeps the money, but a further payment, known as a counter-insurance, ensures that it is repaid to a named beneficiary. The advantage of these policies, which may be taken out for almost any sum, is that the premiums are tax deductible. They are therefore specially suitable for persons earning high salaries.

Additional insurance may be obtained with the payment of extra premiums; after an accidental death the capital paid to the beneficiary may be doubled or tripled; if the insured becomes an invalid he need no longer pay premiums, receives a regular income, and also payment of the capital sum assured in advance. Insurance of this type may also be applied to members of a group, such as executives in the same firm, or members of the same profession, doctors, journalists, etc.

Private health policies make up the deficiencies of the French Health Service, and extra retirement policies add to the State pension (see chapter 10). There are also a myriad other types of insurance policy which can be taken out. The Pope's visit to Lyon was one such; in case of his accidental death, or assassination, a sum of money was to be paid to the Vatican sufficient to cover the expenses of holding the Conclave to elect a new Pope. Other insurees include pop stars, athletes, actors in plays and films, ships, aeroplanes, sporting equipment, and animals – more especially racehorses, valuable farm stock, and pedigree dogs and cats.

After all this, it should be pointed out that the insurance profession in France is subject to considerable criticism, the most informed being published in a special number of the consumer magazine *Que Choisir* (equivalent of the British *Which?*) in January, 1987, just before the Assur/Expo Insurance Fair which was held in Paris in February. I am told that it was not as successful as that held in 1986 and has since been combined with an annual computer exhibition. *Que Choisir* pointed out twenty traps into which policy holders can fall, actively encouraged by the companies who prefer to lose clients rather than money. The first concerned an increase in premium of 30 per cent, the second a change in the contract without informing the person insured, the third a refusal to cancel a policy, refusal to compensate a car accident when a member of the family of the policy holder was driving, and refusal to carry out the terms of a policy designed to ensure payment of a bank loan to purchase a house, if the borrower became ill. Eight traps concerned car insurance, three insurance against theft, three damage to the policy holder's dwelling; these were specifically covered, in theory, by a comprehensive policy. The final trap was that of non-compensation for an accident, when the insurance company had also insured the person who caused the accident. The UFC (*Union Fédérale de Consommateurs* - Federal Union of Consumers), publishers of *Que Choisir*, has started a league for the rights of the insured, whose purpose is to fight to defeat the reprehensible tactics of insurance companies. The League may be contacted at 13 rue de Turbigo, 75002 Paris (Tel: 43 48 55 48).

Many of these traps can be avoided by being forewarned, by making it abundantly clear at the outset against what precise risks the prospective client wishes to be insured, and then reading the resultant policy with extreme care, drawing attention to anomalies, and insisting on their correction. The insurance company wants to stay in business too. It pays to shop around for a suitable policy, with a company which is perhaps prepared to write certain clauses to suit the client.

The foundation of the League, best described as 'the League Against Insurance Abuses', is an excellent example of the awareness that exists in France of the problems of daily life. Abuses need correcting, a new road or railway is necessary, and they are corrected or built. Life is a continuous and stimulating struggle; sometimes the bad guys win, but, in a social context, the good guys do so more often. The conflict itself keeps the protagonists on their toes, and, in the end, reforms are successfully applied to abuses.

11

Children, Schooling, Marriage and Divorce

Children are encouraged and welcomed, because the French birth rate is static, even regressive. Any female resident in France can benefit from State help, from the time that she goes for the first compulsory medical examination before the end of the third month of pregnancy. The other medical examinations required are during the sixth month, the first half of the eighth month, and the first half of the ninth month. All medical expenses involved in pregnancy have been wholly paid for by the State since July 1978.

To obtain pre- and post-natal allowances, the pregnant woman must send to the Family Allowances Office (*Caisse d'Allocations Familiales*), of the city or *département* in which she lives, the appropriate sheet from the maternity booklet (*carnet de maternité*) which will be given to her at the first examination. The payments are made monthly from the fourth month of pregnancy until the baby is three months old, amounting therefore to nine monthly payments. The amount, in February 1990, was about 890Fr per month.

When the baby is born, the birth must be registered at the local town hall, usually by production of the birth certificate issued by the hospital or nursing home in which it took place. A health booklet (*carnet de santé*) will then be provided; the child must have three compulsory medical examinations, the first during the eight days following birth, either in the hospital, or at home by a visiting pediatric nurse, during the ninth or tenth month, and during the 24th or 25th month.

Family allowances are paid to families with two or more children, on a monthly basis until the youngest child is 17, or 20 if she or he is in apprenticeship or in higher education. In February 1990 these amounted to about 620Fr per month for two children and 1,418Fr for three. Pre- and post-natal payments, and allowances for second and subsequent children are made regardless of personal income. Other payments are subject to a means test. These include a *complément familial* (extra family help) of 701Fr per month per child when there are three or more in the family. This system has operated since the end of 1987. Normally, the amounts paid per month for all types of allowances are readjusted twice a year, on January 1st and July 1st.

Children are almost always born in hospitals or nursing homes (*cliniques*); it is very rare to have a baby at home, as neither doctors nor midwives are willing to attend births there. Occasionally a newspaper article recounts the unusual delivery of a baby in a taxi, an ambulance, or by the firemen (*les pompiers*) because there was not time to get to the hospital, but this is the exception. All firemen receive training in elementary obstetrics just in case. Hospital or nursing home accommodation should be reserved as soon as the pregnancy is known, and residence at the time of birth ascertained.

All fathers are entitled to 3 days paid leave during the 15 days before or after the baby's birth (or adoption, where this occurs). A separate allowance is paid to single parents to help them with expenses: this normally goes to mothers, but occasionally to fathers.

Working women are entitled to 16 weeks paid leave, 6 weeks before the birth and 10 weeks afterwards. They are obliged to take a minimum of 8 weeks, and cannot be dismissed from their jobs for reasons of pregnancy – there are, indeed, well attested tales of unsatisfactory female employees becoming pregnant simply in order to avoid dismissal. No distinction is made between married and unmarried mothers: the full resources of the State are called upon to assist the unmarried mother. It is possible for either parent to obtain up to 2 years' unpaid leave to bring up a child or children; this is known as *congé parental*, and can be obtained if the person has worked for at least a year in the same enterprise before requesting it, and if there are more than 100 employees. This 2 year period gives the right to 1 year's seniority.

Once the mother decides to return to work, she has to consider how the child can be looked after during the day. There are the *crèches collectives*, usually run by the commune, for between thirty and sixty children, and *mini-crèches* which are the same but take fewer children. These all have qualified staff, as must private institutions known as *crèches familiales*. Individual baby minders (*assistantes maternelles*) must be licensed by the local social security office, which specifies the number of children she may accept, usually no more than four. If she is totally unqualified, she is strongly encouraged to follow a course of professional further education.

Hours of the larger crèches are normally, from 07.00 to 19.00; the smaller ones, and those with *assistantes maternelles* are more flexible, according to parents' needs. Fees are paid according to family incomes; usually, family allowances cover most of the outlay. The *halte-garderie*, or play group, is for children aged up to six, and permits mothers to leave children for shorter times, so that they can meet, and play with other children, whilst the mother does her errands unencumbered. There is also the *au pair* system, described in Part 1, chapter 3.

At the age of three, children go to the *école maternelle* (nursery school), the normal hours here being 09.00 to 12.00 and 14.00 to 16.00. The children may have lunch at school by arrangement, and be accepted for day care outside these hours, to fit in with paternal work schedules. The *école maternelle* itself is free, but the extra hours must be paid for. The youngest children at the *école maternelle* rest after lunch and have the same kind of care that would be expected in the home.

Vaccination is free and compulsory against tuberculosis (BCG), at the end of the first month of life. A multiple vaccination called *Tetracoque* against whooping cough, tetanus, diphtheria and polio is administered between the 3rd and 5th month, with two boosters, one at 15 months, and the other at 6 years. After that, polio and tetanus protection should be renewed every five years. ROR is free, and advisable, though not compulsory, between the ages of 14 and 18 months; this protects against mumps, measles, and German measles (rubella).

Primary school begins for all children at the age of 6, and continues until 11. In most places 'leisure centres' will take care of them between 16.30 and 18.30 on Wednesdays (which are free days for almost all schoolchildren in France), and during school holidays. Some communes have organised clubs for 13-17 year olds, where appropriate sports and hobbies are organised; elsewhere they may be left on their own, which is where delinquency may begin.

In Levallois Perret, one of the nearer suburbs of Paris, on the edge of the Périphérique, the system has been carried one step further; the town council issues a pamphlet proclaiming 'Pour la premiere fois en France è votre disposition, un Miniclub de Nuit' (For the first time, an overnight Mini-club at your service). Twice a week, on Tuesdays and Fridays, children may be left overnight, from 19.30 to 08.00, so that the parents can go out for the evening. Since this service costs 120Fr per night for everyone, most parents cannot avail themselves of it too often. A night's subscription would certainly make a thoughtful present.

Secondary Schooling
Five years of secondary education are compulsory for all children between the ages of 11 and 16; the more academically inclined will go on to a *lycée* to prepare for the *baccalauréat* at the age of 18, in the *cycle long*. This used to be taken in two sections in consecutive years, *première at deuxième partie*, but these have now been combined into one. There are various options in subjects; generally the *Baccalauréat C*, which consists principally of science and maths, is the most highly valued, and the *Baccalauréat A* (history and literature) having the least prestige. *Bachéllers*, as the young people who win this diploma are known, normally continue to higher education, of which more later, although some leave and go to work, especially if there is a family firm to join.

It is possible, at any time during the years of secondary education, to transfer from a practical to an academic section, or vice-versa; the transition classes are known as *classes passerelles* (corridor classes). The five year *cycle court* (short programme) ends with the award of a certificate of secondary education, the *Brevet*, or else a *Certificat d'Aptitude Professionel* (Certificate of Professional Ability) in various vocational subjects, such as plumbing, carpentry, technical drawing, dressmaking, etc, for some of which there are said to be few openings. Unemployment amongst unqualified school leavers is certainly a problem in France, as in Britain. The French, also, are even more reluctant than the British to leave home, or move house, in search of work.

Both primary and secondary education in France are totally centralised, and have been since the time of Napoleon. The syllabuses are the same in all schools of the same kind, and the textbooks are normally known, bought and even studied in advance. This is astonishing for anyone used to the divergences of school and County Education authorities in Britain; the national Ministry of Education makes all these decisions and does not expect them to be questioned. There is the advantage that children moving from one school to another within the French educational system can pick up where they left off, with minimum disruption. There are, of course, different types of secondary schools: C.E.S. (*Collèges d'Education Sécondaire* – Colleges of Secondary Education), from 15 onward *Lycées* (Grammar Schools), and *Lycées Techniques* for such subjects as agriculture and home economics. *Lycées* in country districts where people are drawn from a wide area take weekly boarders who go home for the weekend.

Most private schools have religious or experimental (eg Rudolf Steiner) affiliations, and enough parents feel strongly about them to have organised mass demonstrations in Paris in 1983, when the socialist government under Mitterand threatened to stop paying teachers in private schools. Catholic education is still quite influential, particularly in the provinces.

There are also some *cours privés* for students of 16+; these are much like private sixth form colleges, and are destined for students from reasonably prosperous families who a) need extra coaching for the *baccalauréat*, or b) who want a particular subject not available at the local *lycée*, or c) those who must be kept out of mischief until they go to do their military service at the age of 18. This is compulsory for boys (although girls may now join the armed forces as well) and lasts between 12 months and 2 years, depending on the branch chosen.

Further Education

After secondary comes higher education, which exists at two levels, the universities being on the lower level. All students holding a *baccalauréat* are admitted to the arts, and some science faculties. The weeding out takes place thereafter, during the first two years when they prepare a DEUG (*Diplôme d'Etudes Universitaires Générales* – Diploma in General University Studies), before going on to a specialisation. Up to 70 per cent of students are said to drop out by the end of these two years. It must be remembered that there is no tutorial system and very little supervision of students' work. They attend lectures and classes as they wish, and their only obligation is to pass the end-of-year exams, one retake normally being allowed in October. A second failure means departure. The next year is spent in getting a *licence* (BA), and two more assure a *maîtrise* (MA). *Doctorats* (PhD) are awarded on two levels: *doctorat de 3ème cycle*, in which some original research is encapsulated in a thesis, and *doctorat d'Etat* – this normally being the culmination of a lifetime's research by an acknowledged authority in a particular field.

These designations apply to general education: schools of medicine, dentistry, and pharmacy are attached to certain universities, and entry to them is by means of a *baccalauréat C*, and the candidate being placed in the top 25 per cent. It is even harder to get into veterinary school; there are four in France, the best known being at Maisons Alfort just outside Paris, and here there is a stiff competitive entrance exam.

The subject of competitive exams brings us to the upper level of higher education; the Grandes Ecoles, a system unique to France. These are professional schools of a very high calibre, which produce the technocrats who run the country. Admission is by *concours*, competitive examinations for a limited number of places. Preparation for these takes two to three years after the *baccalauréat*, and requires both talent and extremely hard work; certain *lycées*, such as Louis-le-Grand and Jeanson de Sailly in Paris, have preparatory classes. The most famous is Polytéchnique, known as 'L'X', a college of engineering founded in 1794 to produce well-trained military engineers. It is still a military establishment, and the students (including girls since 1972) have the rank of military officers. On official occasions they wear an extremely handsome uniform. 'L'X' moved out of Paris to Palaiseau, south of the city, in 1976, and has some very impressive buildings. Military discipline obtains in attending classes and producing assignments: unfortunately the architect who designed the Palaiseau campus forgot to include an examination hall, so that students have had to write their internal exams on the honour system in their own study bedrooms. Those who intend to study law, economics, medicine, or pharmacy in a university must normally be in the top 25 per cent of their Baccalaureate year at secondary school. At the end of their four years of specialised subject study they will take the exam for the *Certificat d'Aptitude Pédagogique à l'Enseignement Sécondaire* generally known as the CAPES, and have done most of the work for the *agrégation*, an extremely difficult competitive exam which is the highest open to teachers in France; once it has been obtained, teachers receive tenure. It is possible, but even more difficult to work for the *agrégation* whilst teaching, and after obtaining a university degree in the subject. Here the failure rate is even higher.

Primary teachers, known as *instituteurs*, attend the *Ecole Normale* in their département, and the local entrance examination which they must pass, after obtaining a DEUG which requires two years of university, is not excessively difficult.

Finally, the CNRS (*Conseil Nationale de la Recherche Scientifique* – National Council for Scientific Research) recruits qualified researchers in all subjects; places are not limited to French citizens, although candidates should have had at least a part of their education in France and know the language well. Here it is important to know the right people, in addition to possessing original ideas and research ability.

Marriage and Marriage Settlements

Nowadays it is the fashion for four out of ten couples to live together before getting married, but it is quite wrong to suppose that marriage as an institution is threatened because of this. This prenuptial cohabitation (which usually lasts about two years) has its limits; only one in ten couples has a child, and pregnancy is usually followed by marriage which in the case of 70 to 80 per cent is celebrated in a church, although in the ordinary way most of these people never attend church services.

Usually this kind of cohabitation is looked upon as a trial. Only 7 per cent are actually opposed to the idea of marriage as a permanency. It is believed that there are fewer unmarried couples today than there were in the nineteenth century, when many uneducated people did not bother to get married at all.

However, the law has been amended since 1978 to give almost equal rights to the unmarried who have the same legal status as a married couple if they sign a declaration 'on their honour' that they are living together 'totally and permanently'. This informal union is recognised by the State as *un etat de concubinage*, best translated as being a common law spouse, and the *mairie* (town hall) of the commune in which the couple live will provide a (free) certificate to that effect that the couple is living in this way, if they present themselves to request it, with proof of identity, and of a joint address (normally indicated on the identity card). They must also provide two witnesses who are unrelated to the couple or to each other.

The advantages of the certificate are that a 50 per cent reduction can be obtained for rail travel for one partner, and the State health insurance of one can be used to benefit the other, both for medical and maternity care. If the couple have a child and both recognise it, they will receive a *livret de famille*; they may also have a joint bank account, though not a joint tax return. Since 1970 parental authority is normally exercised by the mother, even when both parents have recognised the children as being theirs. The common law spouse is only at a disadvantage when the other partner dies; he or she can only inherit the amount allowed to a non-relative, and must pay the full death duty on this. On the other hand, a sum known as *capital-décès* (death payment) is paid after the death of any person registered with the social security and not receiving the old age pension. This amounts to three months of the last salary, if they were still employed, or on sick leave, at the time of death. Here the common law spouse, defined as 'any person living under the same roof as the deceased, and dependent upon him or her', may well be the first beneficiary.

There is no longer any social stigma attached to this way of life, and it is also very common when both partners have been married once, and do not wish to risk a second divorce. The status of the children is safeguarded, and this intermediate state between a bachelor existence and marriage seems to suit many people very well. Of course, the Church fulminates against it, but practising Catholics are now a minority in France (see chapter 15, *France Today*).

In France legal marriage is a State affair; religious ceremonies are permissible, but optional, and depend solely upon the affiliations and inclinations of those who contract them. To be properly married, it is necessary for the *maire* or his deputy, to officiate at a secular tying of the knot. Which *maire*? might be the first question. *Answer*: the *maire* of the commune in which either the bride or the groom resides, or that of their parents. Some communes accept the holiday home of parents or close relatives, so that a country wedding is possible.

The legal age of marriage is 18 years for males and 15 for females. A dispensation may be permitted for younger people, with parental consent, for example in the event of a pregnancy. If there has been a previous marriage, it should have been dissolved at least 300 days previously where the woman is concerned so as to be sure that she is not pregnant. A medical certificate of non-pregnancy may replace part of this delay.

The date for the *mairie* ceremony should be booked at least three months ahead of time, and both partners should have, separately, medical examinations at least a month beforehand. Armed with their medical certificates, they ask the authorities to publish the banns. This is done by affixing a notice on the appropriate board within (or sometimes outside) the town hall, so that it can be confirmed that no obstacle to the marriage exists. At this time proof of identity and of residence should be produced, as well as the *notaire*'s certificate if a marriage contract has been drawn up. Names and addresses of the witnesses (one or two for each partner) must be given. Here the regulations state that if the couple cannot produce any witnesses themselves, the *maire*'s office is responsible for finding them. In practice it is possible to get married without so much delay, but all the formalities as outlined above must be carried out, and the banns announced. The time of the ceremony will be allotted by the *maire* at the time most convenient to the municipal authorities.

Persons who are widowed or divorced must provide documentary evidence of their status. Foreigners who are not EC citizens must produce their residence permits (*carte de séjour*), and if the future spouse is not of French nationality, those serving in the armed forces must obtain permission from their superior officers.

No official expenses are involved in all these formalities, except for the medical examination and fees for the *notaire*. However, it is the custom for the *maire* to arrange a collection in aid of local charities after the wedding ceremony, if the couple can afford it. Women are not obliged to change their surnames upon marriage, but they may if they wish, add their husband's name to their own. The husband may do the same (legislation of July, 1986). Nowadays a woman usually keeps her own name – which of course is that of her father – in her professional life, and uses her husband's in matters affecting them both. Thus: 'Anne and Jean Dupont request the pleasure of your company, etc. . .' *or* 'Anne Duterre, Madame Jean Dupont. . .'

The *livret de famille* (family record book), an official document, is given to a couple at the time of their civil marriage, and to an unmarried mother when her child is born. It is a register of births, marriages, and deaths within the family, and each generation possesses one.

The French are much concerned with acquiring property, particularly buildings and land. The legal system does its best to ensure that they keep it, particularly within a family. The civil contract of marriage is made between two persons of opposite sexes, who agree to live and to have children together. Where property is concerned there are five main possibilities, four of which have to be specified by a contract drawn up by, and signed before a *notaire* ahead of the marriage ceremony. This legislation has been valid since February, 1966.

The system normally adopted does not need a special contract. It is known as the *régime de la communauté d'acquêts*, or system of mutual acquisition. Each partner considers as his or her personal property that which has been acquired before the marriage, or during it by gift or inheritance. Common ownership applies only to that which has been purchased for joint use during the period of marriage.

Each partner is solely responsible for his or her own debts, with the exception of those contracted for the education of the children, or maintenance of the joint household, for which both are liable. Either partner can be sole administrator of the common property, but cannot give any away without the consent of the other. Neither can one alone sell, give in usufruct (to enable the use of income therefrom) or use as a guarantee: real estate, businesses, or working land, which are jointly held.

Of the four arrangements requiring a specific contract, the first is:

(1) *Régime de la communauté de meubles et acquêts* (system of common holding of movable and immovable property).

Here, each partner keeps as personal property all that which he or she owned before the marriage, and that received as a gift or inherited during the marriage. However, both partners may decide to acquire joint property, and to administer jointly every-thing that they own, so that the signature of both is required for any transaction.

(2) The second is the *Régime de séparation des biens* (system of separate ownership).
Each partner remains totally independent from the legal and fi-nancial point of view. There is no community property, and each one does as they wish with their separate possessions.

(3) The third is the *Régime de participation aux acquêts* (system of sharing property acquired).
The general rules are the same as in (2) except that, at the end of the marriage, whether by death or divorce, the survivor, or each partner of the dissolved marriage, has the right to a half share of the other person's acquisitions, being the difference between that possessed at the beginning and at the end of the marriage. This excludes property received as a gift or inherited, by one or the other individually.

(4) The fourth is the *Régime de la communauté universelle* (sys-tem of complete common ownership). Here all property is held in common, and both partners give up the right to personal property, except perhaps for clothes and toothbrushes.

The fees charged by *notaires* for drawing up these contracts vary according to the amount and the type of property specified in the contract. Variations exist for each type of contract, and it is possible, after two years of married life, to modify or alter it, if this is required in the interest of the family.

During the marriage each partner may sign separately any contracts which concern children's education or household main-tenance; each debt thus entered into requires the other partner to participate, except where it is obviously excessive, or involves credit purchase.

Each partner may open and operate a bank account for their own benefit, once the joint household expenses are taken care of. The death of the other partner cannot block this. On the other hand, neither partner can sell, nor revoke the lease of, their joint dwelling, nor sell the furniture, even if it is the personal property of one or the other, without the other partner's consent.

Both husband and wife have the same rights of administration and of the disposal of property held in common. Under certain circumstances one can obtain a mortgage against the other as security for property alienated. These arrangements are familiar to married couples in the UK or elsewhere, but in France they are more firmly incorporated into the legal system.

Death

Now the material problems surrounding death, which must be dealt with by the survivors – family, friends, or strangers. If death takes place at home, after an illness, and is therefore expected, an undertaker will be summoned to take care of the body, and the local doctor in order to provide a death certificate and thus obtain *le permis d'inhumer* (burial permission). The local *mairie* should be informed, so that the records can be kept up to date. An entry is also made in the appropriate *livret de famille*. The same formalities take place in hospital, but if families wish to take the body home before the funeral ceremony, it is better to arrange for an understanding doctor to sign an exit permit as if the person were still alive, and to arrange ambulance transport.

If, on the other hand, death results from an accident, murder, or suicide, the police or *gendarmerie* must be informed, and their official doctor (*médecin légiste*) only can give the *permis d'inhumer*.

In France, considerable importance is still attached to funerals. Neighbours in a village or small town will be expected to attend the ceremony even if this is some distance away. Family tombs, usually elaborate, are tended carefully, and their ownership handed down from one generation to another. At the *Toussaint* (All Saints' Day) and the *Fête des Morts* (November 1 and 2) people visit family graves and place flowers, usually large pots or bunches of chrysanthemums, upon them. This, incidentally, is why chrysanthemums are rarely seen in houses or used as decoration; they are flowers for the dead rather than for the living. Generally speaking, wives are expected to visit and tend their husbands' graves, as children are their parents', on a regular basis, and if they live elsewhere they make the pilgrimage at least once a year. This has little to do with religious affiliation or practice, it seems to be a survival of a much more ancient custom. In the country graveyards surround the Roman (Catholic) church, or are on the outskirts of the village, with a part reserved for non-Catholic or non-religious funerals; in the city, cemeteries are municipal enterprises.

Because of this attachment to physical remains, autopsies, the donation of bodies for scientific purposes, and that of organs such as eyes and kidneys, which can be of use to someone else, are organised rather differently than in other countries. In the UK, for example, printed on all driving licences is: 'I request that after my death my kidneys, eyes, heart, liver, pancreas be use for transplantation; or any part of my body be used for the treatment of others. Delete (in whole or part) if not applicable.' In France, on the other hand, persons wishing to give 'spare parts' after death, should carry a donor card to make this clear. It may be obtained from: La Fédération française pour le don d'organes et de tissus humains, Cité Joliot Curie, route d'Enghien, 95100 Argenteuil. Tel: (1) 39 82 38 98. Since 31 March 1978 all hospitals have the right to take the organs of deceased persons, unless the person before death, or the family, states clearly that they do not wish this to be done. The possession of a donor card is irrefutable proof that the deceased did wish this, and prevents any misunderstanding with the family.

The donation of a body is quite a different matter; it is necessary to write to the medical school nearest to the usual place of residence, which will then indicate the conditions to be fulfilled. Normally a financial contribution is required, for 'expenses'. The regulations further specify the right of a medical school to refuse a body if it has no use for it. In Paris and the suburbs apply to: Le Centre des Dons de Corps, Faculté de Médecine, 45 rue des Saints Pères, 75006 Paris. A minimum contribution of 450Fr must be made.

In some communes a particular undertaker, *pompes funèbres*, the only one permitted to operate therein, is allotted a municipal concession. This is more frequent in the country. This is a virtual monopoly, and since there is no competition, prices tend to be high. Edouard Léclerc of the LeClerc Supermarket chain is attempting to alter this. Elsewhere the hospital, or doctor, can advise. In the case of an accident, the gendarmerie are usually most helpful. Four classes of funeral exist, No 1 being the most expensive and elaborate, and No 4 being the cheapest; the undertakers arrange with the local clergy when their services are needed. In Catholic ceremonies, a collection is usually taken at the end for the benefit of the church. The undertaker's bill must be paid *before* the funeral, but bank and Post Office accounts, blocked because of the death, will release up to 10,000Fr, to be paid directly to the undertaker, to meet his bill. You can, of course, take out an insurance policy for this purpose. Paupers are buried, in individual graves, in the local cemetery, at municipal expense, but close relatives are expected to contribute from their own pockets if they are able to do so.

Funeral arrangements for foreigners depend upon their wishes, their financial circumstances, and their insurance policies. Some may wish to have their bodies transported back home; others are content to be buried, or cremated, wherever convenient. Cremation is possible in France, though not every town has a crematorium; transport to one can be arranged, and the cost of cremation is about half that of conventional burial. However, as far as possible, some provision should be made in advance to ensure desired arrangements for the body.

Death is normally followed by division of the deceased's property. This must be done according to the law, and inheritance laws in France are quite different to those that obtain in Britain, or in the US for that matter.

It is impossible to disinherit children in France, except by dying totally destitute, bestowing all one's possessions in one's lifetime, or by means of the *viager* system, explained below. Children have the right to the *réserve héréditaire* (hereditary share); this means that when anyone makes a will, half of the property must be left to an only child, ⅔ divided between two, and ¾ between 3 or more. This means that only 50 per cent, 33⅓ per cent, or 25 per cent may be left 'freely' to husband, wife, or any third party, whether they be person or institution. It explains, incidentally, why advertisements are never seen in France urging people to leave money to charitable organisations in their wills, as is frequently done in Britain or the US. Some tax deductions are available for charitable gifts made during the donor's lifetime.

When a person dies intestate, the children divide the property between them in equal proportions – there is no primogeniture in France, either. Since there is no longer a monarchy, titles of nobility are purely honorific; nevertheless, all the male children of a comte or marquis have the right to use the title. Their sisters and wives can be known as 'Comtesse' or 'Marquise'. The surviving spouse of a person who dies intestate is entitled only to life income from 25 per cent of the property if there are children, and 50 per cent if there are none. If there is no husband or wife, and no children either, the closest relatives, usually parents, brothers, sisters, and then cousins in descending order, divide the property between them.

To emphasise this principle, death duties are quite low for children and spouses (on their permitted percentages). They vary between 5 and 40 per cent, this last being levied on a sum greater than 11,200,000Fr. For brothers and sisters they are between 35 and 40 per cent according to the amount left; for more distant relatives, such as cousins, 55 per cent and mere non-relatives 60 per cent whatever the sum. A certain amount is tax-exempt; here again the favouring of the family is obvious: 275,000Fr are tax exempt for the surviving spouse, parents, and children. For non-relatives the exemption is 10,000Fr. *Notaires'* fees are also considerably higher for non-relatives. Conclusion: make gifts to outsiders during your lifetime, if you want them to benefit.

Obviously, property or a business owned and operating in France is subject to French laws concerning its disposal by testament; the formation of a company, with different shareholders, is often a good idea, to ensure continuity, not necessarily within the family. *Caveat emptor.*

There is, however, a means of ensuring that the surviving spouse gets a little more than the notoriously small amount permitted by law; this is called *donation entre époux* (gift between spouses), and is a legal document enabling him or her to choose, at the time of the other's death, between:

full ownership of that proportion of the property which he or she can leave as they wish (50, 33⅓, or 25 per cent)
or 25 per cent of the property absolutely, and the rest as life income (usufruct)
or life income of all the property, with reversion to the children and other legal heirs.

The choice will be made according to the most suitable circumstances at the time. No real estate can be sold, except that owned absolutely, without the agreement of the children, as they have a reserve interest in it. This *donation* can be revoked if made during the marriage; it is irrevocable if made as part of the marriage contract.

A *donation partage* (division of gift) can be made jointly by parents or grandparents during their lifetimes, so that they can decide who gets what, or withhold certain objects from unappreciative offspring. This donation can also be revoked.

The *viager* arrangement (life income against alienation of capital) is the only way in which parents can prevent children from inheriting; at the same time it makes old people independent of their offspring, often a most desirable state. This arrangement consists of selling property, usually a house or apartment, to a third party, on condition that the vendor may continue to occupy it during his or her lifetime, against an annual income to be agreed upon, and paid monthly or quarterly. Sometimes a lump sum known as a *bouquet* is paid at the time of the sale; the annual sum paid is correspondingly reduced. The total amount is estimated by means of actuaries' tables, and depends upon the age of the vendor and the value of the property. Some magazines contain columns devoted to *ventes en viager* (*viager* sales), with such sinister details as '2 têtes' – 70 and 75 years old. These sales are often made by a couple for the benefit of the survivor, either husband or wife. He or she then has the right to occupy the property until death.

The purchase of property in this fashion is a frequent form of investment in France, and means that those who have worked hard to earn their money can enjoy it undisturbed in old age. Normally, the occupiers are responsible during their lifetime for all expenses concerning the property, whether it be re-papering the sitting room, or re-roofing the house.

Sometimes a *vente viagère* is made to a child; when there is more than one the arrangement is legally regarded as a *donation partage*, *unless* the consent of all the children has been obtained at the time that it is made.

Disagreements over property and inheritance form, alas, one of the less pleasant aspects of French life, but this is sometimes to the advantage of foreigners, especially if they wish to buy a house with several heirs and no immediate occupiers that is in a remote country area. A sum of money can always be divided; a house cannot, and joint occupation frequently leads to friction. Moreover, if children inherit their parents' property, they also inherit their debts, which may often be municipal taxes owed to the commune. A deal that will rid them of accumulated taxes, and give them a little cash too, is often welcome.

12
The French Background

France Today can only be understood if a little is known about France Yesterday, and more particularly France in the nineteenth century. France was a monarchy until 1792, and the violent end of Louis XVI the following year so shocked most of the French people, that the establishment of the Consulate in 1799, and then the Empire ruled by Napoleon Bonaparte in 1804, came almost as a relief. Napoleon's military victories brought prestige and wealth to France, as well as uniting the European powers against him; the formation of large armies for the Napoleonic wars meant employment, food, and a chance of plunder for the soldiers, most of whom were of peasant origin, and whose traditional lives had been interrupted by the Revolution. The oppressive absentee landlords to whom the peasants had been obliged to pay taxes, as well as provide forced, unpaid labour were gone, but so were those who traditionally had told them what to do, and had organised the agricultural year. Even the names of the months were changed. Some peasants could do quite well on their own initiative, but most needed guidance. The army provided this, and although many soldiers died in the 1812/1813 retreat from Russia, the war was not on French soil until 1814.

From then on, until after 1870, there was a constant see-saw between monarchists and republicans. At the same time, the Industrial Revolution had taken place, and there was, for the middle class, growing prosperity from manufacturing industry. Colonial expansion, too, made many French people rich. Industry and colonial adventures are not so different as the casual observer might think. Manufacturers needed raw materials and markets for their finished goods, both of which the African and Asian colonies could provide. All the European powers were engaged in colonial competition: Russia in the Far East, Italy in Libya, Spain in Morocco, Germany in Togo and Namibia, Great Britain in India, Africa, and the Far East, and Belgium in the Congo. In fact the Congo territories were annexed by King Leopold of the

Belgians as his personal fief, from which he made a huge fortune, and then left to the Belgian state at his death. Holland acquired possessions in Indonesia, and Denmark some Caribbean islands. France was involved in North Africa, in parts of black Africa, and in South East Asia, with footholds in the Caribbean – Martinique, Guadeloupe, and Guyana; India – Pondichéry; the Indian Ocean – the island of La Réunion, and in the Pacific, *Nouvelle Calédonie* (New Caledonia) and Tahiti. With the exception of Pondichéry, which became part of India in 1956, all these last named are still part of France today, and are known collectively as the DOM/TOM (*Départements d'Outre Mer/Territoires d'Outre Mer*).

Napoleon was finally defeated at Waterloo in 1815; the Restoration government, under two kings who were brothers, Louis XVIII and then Charles X, gradually became more reactionary, with an attempt to return to feudal privileges. The July Revolution of 1830 brought their cousin Louis Philippe to the throne, as a far more liberal monarch. Unfortunately, the influence of his chief adviser, Guizot, led the King to favour the rising and affluent *bourgeoisie* over the workers, who, becoming increasingly exploited, reacted with the Revolution of 1848. Then, until 1852, there was a republican government, that seemed to fulfil the hopes of universal suffrage and shared prosperity, but too many vested interests – of landowners, industrialists, and the Church – were at stake. Louis-Napoleon Bonaparte, nephew of the Emperor Napoleon I, became Prince-President in 1851, and Emperor – as Napoleon III – in 1852. During his reign France became richer as business flourished, and the basic infrastructure of government was strengthened. Political life became freer, and parliamentary rule was set up, but the Emperor's foreign adventures led to the Franco-Prussian war and the defeat in 1870 that resulted in the loss of Alsace and Lorraine. A good many people, mainly Alsacians, not wishing to become German, settled in Algeria and ran large farms there with considerable success.

France had no more monarchs after 1870. The National Assembly had a monarchist majority from 1871 to 1875, and would have restored the legitimate heir, the Comte de Chambord, under the title of Henri V. However, his foolish insistence upon having the white flag with golden lilies, symbol of France before the Revolution, cost him the throne. The *Tricolor* had already become the French flag, the white representing the monarchy, and the red and blue being the colours of Paris (city and river). The Revolution of 1789 had, of course, begun in Paris. The Comte de Chambord died in 1883, leaving no heir, and never having ruled. The succession passed to the younger, Orléans, branch of the Bourbons, represented today by the Comte de Paris.

The Third Republic lasted from 1871 to 1940. After 1875 it became more radical and more anti-clerical, under the leadership of Léon Gambetta, a lawyer from Cahors, who began as a liberal reformer and became more and more opposed to the *ordre moral* of the monarchist and clerical supporters. The 1876 elections saw the triumph of the Republic, which was never to be seriously questioned again as a form of government. Jules Ferry, a prominent politician between 1879 and 1885, was responsible for setting up the free and compulsory State education system, establishing secondary schools for girls, and bringing in laws to ensure the freedom of the Press and the increased independence of local government. The division between traditional supporters of the Church, and the anti-clerical movement increased; much Church property was secularised, including that of religious orders in 1905.

The fall in the birth rate has been a most serious problem; it fell steadily in the late nineteenth and early twentieth centuries, and then the 1914-1918 war caused the deaths of two million Frenchmen, mostly in trench warfare in eastern and north-eastern France. The country was impoverished by this war, recovery was slow, and hindered by the world economic crisis of 1929-1931. The rise of the Nazis in Germany was not taken sufficiently seriously whilst the Front Populaire, 1936-37, improved the lot of the workers. For the first time they had paid holidays and could not be dismissed on the spot without compensation. The forty hour week was instituted, and the Bank of France nationalised.

The threat of war only gradually became serious; when it broke out in September 1939 nothing much happened for the first few months, and France was convinced that she was adequately defended by the Maginot Line. When the German armies broke through and overran the country in May/June 1940 the French could hardly believe it. The defeat was caused by military unreadiness, and internal political dissensions. The Petain régime established in Vichy was not as unpopular then as it later became. The motto of '*Travail, Famille, Patrie*,' had a certain appeal to a nation shocked by the German occupation. Nevertheless, there was an immediate response to de Gaulle's appeal to join the Free French Forces, based first in Britain and then in North Africa. The Resistance in France became strong, and contributed greatly to the German defeat.

After 1945 France took on a new lease of life; the Fourth Republic had an old country to rebuild, and a new form of government to establish. Various far-reaching social reforms were carried out: social security was set up, railways and other public services were nationalised, workers' councils came into being, and development plans were carried out. Higher taxes and increased production paid for this, as did increased exports, particularly to the colonies, or countries within the French 'sphere of influence'. In the 1950s, no-one seems to have foreseen that the market for durable consumer goods is not infinitely extensible; once everyone has a car, a TV set, a refrigerator, a washing machine, and a music centre, a limited quantity of replacements and spare parts only are required each year. Of course, more efficient household machinery is continually being developed, but most of those who own a vacuum cleaner tend to wait until it wears out before buying a new one. There were two prosperous decades, and then expansion slowed up with the first oil crisis in 1973.

Today, the history of France is often seen, by French and foreigners alike, as a series of monuments to both past and future glory. Examples of the past are, in Paris, the Sainte Chapelle, Les Invalides, the Arc de Triomphe, and the Eiffel Tower. In the provinces they include the cathedrals of Chartres and Reims, the Mont St Michel, the Palace of the Popes in Avignon, the *château* of Monségur. Certain nineteenth century reconstructions, such as that of the city of Carcassone, by Viollet le Duc, were carried out in this spirit.

Beginning in the 1960s, the complex of La Défense, just outside the Paris *Péripherique*, has been constructed to become a twenty first century monument. When the Socialists came to power in 1981, work also began to redesign the Louvre museum, with a Perspex pyramid in the central court, and acres of underground exhibition and lecture space. The enormous cost of this modern monument has been borne by the State (or rather the taxpayer), and also by Japanese industrial donors. It was felt that the glory of France – and the encouragement of the tourist trade – required this expenditure. Another success has been in the redevelopment of the Bastille quarter, on the east side of Paris. Here a new opera house has been built, which enhances still further the capital's contribution to the Arts.

For France, the latter part of the twentieth century is much less disturbed and insecure than was the similar period in the nineteenth. A quieter kind of history is happening now; since 1945 there have been various non-violent changes of government, left wing, right wing, and in between, but most have been calm and orderly. The closest to civil disturbance came in 1968, with student demonstrations demanding reforms of the educational system. These were granted, and the students returned to their lecture halls.

The problems of France today are those of Western Europe as a whole: an economic decline manifested by high unemployment, and the failure to adapt old industries to a new world. Labour costs are high in France, as is the employer's share of social insurance, so everything is done to reduce the number of workers employed. Those who desperately need a job often accept 'moonlight' work, with no rights guaranteed. It is also extremely difficult to dismiss employees, however unsatisfactory they may be; this may give them job security, but it makes employers very cautious about taking on new ones. On the other hand, a great deal of the State's resources are spent on unemployment pay – the answer might be more direction of labour to where it is most needed.

In the 1960s industry was still expanding, and extra hands were needed to work in the factories. North Africans were encouraged to come to France and get jobs, and even to bring their families with them. The statistics are interesting: between 1800 and 1936 there were 5 million immigrants to France, and between 1956 and 1984 two million more came. In 1984 it was estimated that 4 million non-French citizens lived in the country, some of whom would become French in due course, some would return to their countries of origin, and some would have children born in France who would thus automatically become French citizens. Now, in 1989, the country could easily dispense with a large number, but as life in their own countries is somewhat less comfortable than in France, most have no desire to leave.

The largest foreign communities in France are Portuguese,

Algerian, Italian, Spanish, followed by smaller numbers of Tunisians, Yugoslavs, Poles, and people from the various French speaking countries of Black Africa: Senegal, Niger, Mali, Burkina Fasso, Chad, Mauretania, etc, in even smaller quantities. There are also many South East Asians, mostly Vietnamese and Laotians, who are quiet, hard-working, have a good command of French, and have managed to assimilate without too much difficulty. The Franco-Polish link is long and honourable, and the Portuguese, Spanish and Italians fit in well enough, coming as they do from the same European Catholic tradition.

The problems arise with the North African Arabs; there are several reasons for this. Firstly, they are all Muslims, and the Islamic way of life is in many ways diametrically opposed to that of France. The French colonial system differed from the British in that the French sought to replace the culture of the colonised with their own, naturally assumed to be superior. The idea was to turn as many Algerians, Senegalese, or Laotians into totally assimilated and educated Frenchmen with a slightly different skin colour. This worked up to a point, but could not include the poorer or less educated; Muslims in particular resented the attempt to denigrate Islamic culture. In Algeria, few French schools taught Arabic, a good deal of land was planted with vineyards which grew grapes to make wine, and all kinds of pork *charcuterie* were available, and their consumption encouraged. Algeria was part of France, divided into three *départements*, and expected to act as did all the others. The same is true of Martinique, Guadeloupe, Réunion, and New Caledonia today.

The majority of North Africans in France came as workers to carry out the dirtiest and most tiresome industrial and cleaning jobs; (they are still the largest proportion of the Métro cleaners in Paris). They were, therefore, at the bottom of the heap and looked down upon by everyone else. Many are illiterate, or have little formal education; they come from remote villages, being recruited by labour contractors who were handsomely paid for their catches. For the workers, France was vast and incomprehensible, the tight family network was no longer there to reassure them, and whilst personal initiative in taking care of themselves and working their way up the industrial ladder was encouraged, any kind of political or trade union involvement was condemned.

The surprising thing has been not that so many of these

workers from the Maghreb have become alienated from their own background, and being unable to fit into French society – usually through lack of education – have turned to crime, but rather that often they turned even more fervently to their religion. Families settled in France sometimes find their brighter children, who go to school and do well, slipping away into the temptations of French life. But just as often these children start to search for their Arabic and Muslim heritage. Many workers live as bachelors, with families back home, whom they visit once a year during their holidays, and they too become more fervent, whilst remaining in the alien land. They realise that if jobs have become scarcer in France, they have become even scarcer in the Maghreb.

The French generally are ignorant of Islamic life and customs – as indeed they are of anything not French. When they do know something about it, it is thought to be strange and alien. There is a certain feeling of guilt – often unconscious – about the inhospitality to these 'strangers in our midst'. As more and more young French people travelling in Muslim countries are hospitably received, they feel ashamed when they remember the indifference and hostility accorded to Muslims back home. Anyone living in France for more than a few weeks can easily observe this phenomenon; it is very much part of France Today.

One final word about the role of the Church in France today. France is nominally a Catholic country, but the priests and bishops in France now have a suitably evangelical lean and hungry look, because the Church is no longer a rich landowner. The great churches and cathedrals of the land are under the wing of the Ministry of Fine Arts and are only operated by the Church. Any structural change, or even repair, must be authorised by the Ministry. About 70 to 80 per cent of Catholic born children are baptised, but a much higher proportion of people who die are buried with a religious ceremony. Fewer are married in church, which is usually to enable the bride to wear a white wedding dress, although only a minority believe in the virtue of the Sacrament.

Protestants are estimated to form 3 per cent of the population, and there are 700,000 Jews, as well as the Christian offshoots known elsewhere – Quakers, Jehovah's Witnesses, Seventh Day Adventists, etc – and the Buddhists. We have already discussed Muslims, the second largest religious community in France after Catholics. In general religious observance is declining, and practising Christians are becoming fewer, although few people are atheists – a belief in God is general but vague. There are, however, oases of the faith, in communities such as the Jesuit house of Les Fontaines in Chantilly – described in its brochure as a *Centre Culturel* so as not to scare off the pagans who attend seminars there on all kinds of subjects; the headquarters of the Prado order in Lyon; and the Protestant ecumenical centre at Taizé in Burgundy. The world famous shrine of Our Lady at Lourdes in the Pyrénées has an enormous number of visitors, most being the sick in search of a miraculous cure, all conventional medicine having failed. Recently the French Bishops' Conference met there and issued a statement condemning racial persecution and the evils of poverty, and gave positive practical advice on how to overcome both.

The Stock Market slump on 19 October 1987 was not such a total disaster in France as it was in the USA, Britain, or Japan. Speaking very generally, the French put their savings into land and buildings, sometimes in businesses as sleeping partners, or in municipal bonds, and the share transactions of individuals are carried out with 'pocket money' which they can normally afford to lose. If they make money they buy a new car, smart clothes, or an expensive holiday – all luxuries without which it is possible to live. Today unemployment is as high as ever, business opportunities are lessening, and money is much tighter. But people continue to eat well, improve their houses, and to run the businesses that have been there for a long time.

France Today does seem to be looking with some enthusiasm towards France Tomorrow. New museums, railways, and leisure centres, not to mention the Channel Tunnel, will adorn the beginning of the twenty first century, and enhance the quality of French life, or so the planners hope.

Appendix A
Bibliography

This is a list of works to which we are particularly indebted, and which may help readers to follow up subjects we have only referred to briefly:

Dudley, James W. *1992, Strategies for the Single Market* (Kogan Page)
Hunter, Rob. *Walking in France* (Oxford Illustrated Press)
Lyall, Archibald. *Companion Guide to The South of France* (Collins)
Neillands, Robin. *Walking Through France* (Collins)
Thomas, Bill. *The Legal Beagle Goes to France* (Quiller Press)
Turner, Anthony. & Brown, Christopher. *Burgundy* (Batsford)
Rowe, Vivian. *The Loire* (Eyre Methuen)
White, Freda. *Three Rivers of France*
  Ways of Aquitaine
  West of the Rhône (Faber)
Worthington, *Discovering the Vineyards of France* (Ward)
Zeldin, Theodore. *The French* (Flamingo)

Maps, Guides & Handbooks
IGN (Institut Geographique National), *IGN Green*, 1cm-10km, good for footpaths
IGN two large scale series 1cm-0.25km, for walkers and climbers, all from McCarta, 122 King's Cross Road, London WC1 9DS, or at newsagents in France
Michelin Route Planning Map 911, motorways and alternative routes, *Map No 989*, red 1cm-110km. *Regional Maps*, yellow 1cm-2km, *Michelin Motoring Atlas*, paperback £7.95, hardback, £16.95. *Paris, Atlas*, No. 11. Also from McCarta. Plus *Red Michelin Guide*, restaurants, town plans.
Michelin Green Guides, 19 regions in French, 9 in English; *Michelin: Camping, Caravanning, France*
Logis de France, out March annually (send 80p stamps – 1989).

Gîtes de France Official Handbook, £3, including membership fee and free booking service, both from French Government Tourist Office, 178 Piccadilly, W1V 0AL

Routiers Guide to France (Routiers, McDonald Orbis) £6.95, 354 Fulham Road, London, SW10 9UH

Tessa Youell & George Kimball, *French Food and Wine* (Xanadu, Pocket Guide)

Ville à Ville, SNCF Timetable 'Indicateur'

Shell Guide, France, Edited Edward Young

Monthly Magazines for the Intending Expatriate
LOCATIONS & VENTES, Le Mensuel National de l'Immobilier, Editions Bertrand. National Edition includes Paris, suburbs and some provinces between the 1st and 15th of each month. Regional editions cover Rhône Alpes, Dauphiné-Savoie, Ouest et Midi Mediterranée, about the 1st of each month. 100 pages of property advertisements.

LE PARTICULIER (consumer information) also obtainable on subscription.

House Hunting

Estate Agents in France
Côte D'Azur: John Taylor, 55 La Croisette, 06400 Cannes
John Taylor, 1 Avenue Albert 1er, 06230, St. Jean Cap Ferrat,
  Tel: 93 76 02 38
Dordogne: Keith Wilson, 4 rue du Paris, 24260, Le Bugue, Tel:
  53 07 23 23
Normandy: Simon Hosken, 86, Avenue de la Libération 50400,
  Granville, Tel: 33 51 45 22
South Brittany: Maitre Bernard, Notaires Associés, 56240,
  Plouay, Tel: 97 33 31 48
Touraine: M André Carrete, Agence Immobilière, Tours.
Tours: Century 21, Agence du Parc, 4 Bd de Chinon, 37300
  Joué-les-Tours, Tel: 47 25 12 19
St Lo: Départemental Brochure from Jacques Le Prieur, Maison
  du Département, 50008 St Lo, Normandy
Lot-Tarn et Garonne: M Pierre Passemard, 46170 Flaugnac, Tel:
  65 21 96 05 Fax: 65 21 83 28

Estate Agents with International Links in London
Gerrard Ltd. 280 Earl's Court Road, London SW5 9AS, Tel: 01
  370 4001
Hamptons International, 6 Arlington Street, St. James's, London
  SW1A 1RB, Tel: 01 493 4921
Prudential Property Services, 2 Arlington Close, Wimbledon
  Village, London SW19 5AP
Barbers for Normandy, Brittany, Dordogne, Charente, Tel: 01
  381 0112; France Mediterraneé 645 0773
Andrew Lanauvre & Co, Tel: 01 499 0587
Rutherfords, Tel: 01 351 4454

An increasing number of advertisements for house agents handling French properties is appearing every week in the *Financial
Times* and *The Times*. It should be noted that the best bargains

may well only be those that purchasers can find for themselves on the spot, and there is no real substitute for a house hunting expedition. However, the assistance of a knowledgeable agent will be irreplaceable later in the sale (see *Setting Up House*, chapter 4).

The Loan Position in France
The mortgage position has changed dramatically recently, and there are now more alternatives for raising loans. United Bank of Kuwait wishes to be the first UK based lender to offer French Franc mortgages for the purchase of residential property; the mortgage rate is fluid but will move in line with the Paris Interbank Offered Rate (PIBOR) (9.9 per cent in mid-1989). Banque National de Paris (BNP, c/o 60 Brompton Road, London SW3 1BW) and Société Générale are offering through their UK subsidiaries a choice of mortgages, plus documentation on tax, legal advisers etc. BNP will lend up to 80 per cent of the property value provided your existing commitments are no more than 30 per cent of your world wide income. UCB, the French owned mortgage company offers 70 per cent but will go higher for mortgages in a special class. Interest rates in France are 9.4 per cent, whereas in the UK they are higher (14.15 per cent in August 1989). Certain French banks and institutions, such as Crédit Foncier, will lend up to 80 per cent of the value of a property, taking a mortgage on it as security. They require proof of income to ensure repayment.

British Building Societies are now joining in, and both the Abbey National and the Halifax Building Society have announced that you may take out a second mortgage, but it will be in sterling and secured against your English home.

A recent publication by bankers Crédit Agricole is now published in English. It can be obtained from them in London at Mortgage à la Française, Condor House, 14 St Paul's Churchyard, London EC4. As well as details on finance there is a great deal of other up-to-date information, plus vital advice on the avoidance of legal errors, inappropriate agreements, etc.

Exchange Rates
Exchange rates can shift suddenly while you are buying your property, but for some time have kept within a 10 per cent band. This means that although losses will not be dramatic, you may

still stand to lose a few thousand Francs if there is too much delay while your loan is being converted.

This change in the rates needs watching at every stage of your house purchase particularly if you decide to indulge in large scale renovation or conversion backed by a detailed *devis* (estimate). It is always worth considering paying in advance for a large percentage of the work contracted so that your sterling back-up will be adequate. This makes it more than ever important not to engage in renovations without considerable confidence in your builders or *artisans*.

Of course, the exchange rate might go the other way, so you could be worse off – it is worth getting to know the direction of the fluctuations in the value of the pound, and this can be followed through the *Financial Times*, which also publishes good articles on inflation within the European community, since every expatriate must sooner or later familiarise himself with the movement of money. It is impossible to make long term predictions, but it is possible to recognise periods when acquiring a small fund of Francs could be profitable, as in any case you will be need these to defray expenses in the near future.

Finance and the Law of Inheritance
Expatriates often overlook the fact that in France a simple transfer of property from one spouse to another, under a will, cannot be done, and if an English will already exists it is set aside by the French Inheritance Law aimed at protecting minors. Thus, in the case of joint ownership specifying *en division* , if there are two children, each child automatically inherits one third of the deceased parent's half share. Should there have been a remarriage, a widow might find herself obliged to stay in France because children who actually do not live with her in fact own one sixth of her house, and she cannot afford another.

Luckily, there is a further clause that can be used for joint purchase. This is *en tontine* , which states that the property has been bought jointly with the understanding that it belongs absolutely to the spouse who outlives the other. In fact, this clause has been challenged in the French Civil Court from time to time by children who wish to preserve their rights, but it is regarded as unlikely that the children of foreigners would go to this length to upset their parents' English wills.

All these problems must be discussed openly with your *notaire*, whose knowledge of English may be very limited. A full sized dictionary could be necessary for your first visit, plus the courage to confess ignorance about some of the finer points discussed.

Planning Your Removal
There are few complications about removing your furniture and effects to France – most reputable removals firms now have an international section which is completely trustworthy, and you can profit by their actual experience. Because there appear to be enormous differences in basic charges, modes of packing, collecting etc, you must obtain at least three or four complete estimates before committing yourself in any way. You will need up-to-date knowledge about the position vis-à-vis any probable Customs charges, and it is advisable to make enquiries via the French Consulate General, 24, Rutland Gate, London SW7, Tel: 01 581 5292 about the regulations covering the import of household effects. Do not be content with vague assurances that you are 'allowed' one container load free of all duty. If you will be occupying temporary accommodation to begin with, take the opportunity to convey both valuable and useful articles yourself in an estate car or similar vehicle, and if you are definitely staying for a number of years, also question the wisdom of taking old, outsize furniture, when you can probably sell at auction and buy new on arrival. Meanwhile, make advance enquiries well before your proposed date of departure through Customs Clearance Agents and shipping and forwarding agents, both of whom can be found in the Yellow Pages. Further information can be supplied by HM Customs & Excise, Dorset House, Stamford Street, London SE1 9PS, Tel: 01 928 0533, who will be glad to advise you about the current export controls on antiques over fifty years old, etc.

One tested and approved method of removal is to rent a self-drive van in France, take it back to the UK to pick up furniture and other goods, drive it to the new home, unload and then return it to the nearest office of the hiring company.

If a removals firm is used, experience shows that it is often better to use a French firm and accompany the van to the UK, oversee the loading and then be on the spot to receive the load. Import (to France or anywhere else) is always more complicated than export (from the UK), and a French company can cope better with any hassles.

Cross Channel Ferries

Taking your own car by car ferry is possibly the most practical method when it comes to house-hunting. It is rarely necessary to book in advance if you use shorter crossings, and unless you are taking advantage of the special 'Saver' Fares (and there are remarkably good savings) you can go out by one route and return by another. If you want to go by the longer routes, and hire a cabin, you should book fairly well in advance except in the off season; if you are taking pot luck on the shorter crossings, remember not to choose the most popular sailings of the day.

Probably the easiest ferry to book is Sealink as this can be done through principal BR stations as well as travel centres and travel agents. There are innumerable Dover-Calais and Folkestone-Boulogne crossings, as well as Portsmouth-Cherbourg; the more off-beat Weymouth-Cherbourg (the handy route for West Country people) has the least number. Folkestone-Boulogne, which takes 1hr 50mins, has the extra attraction of a free, really comfortable lounge for motorists only.

P & O Ferries, sailing on the same crossings, plus Portsmouth-Le Havre, (but not Weymouth-Cherbourg), and substituting Dover-Boulogne for Folkestone-Boulogne, also has some luxury motorists' lounges for the payment of a small fee. One interesting thing about P & O is that by becoming a Preference Shareholder you can buy tickets at a considerable discount, but not for the more popular sailings in high season.

Brittany Ferries now sails to St Malo and Caen in Normandy from Portsmouth as well as to Roscoff from Plymouth, but advance booking is required in high season.

Don't forget the Newhaven-Dieppe route, still being marketed by Sealink but now wholly operated by France. It is a good medium-length run that gets you further south. Hoverspeed, Dover-Boulogne, Calais, is another quicker alternative and Sally Line is the sole operator on Ramsgate-Dunkirk.

The alternative is to fly and hire a car on arrival if your house-hunting is to be concentrated in one region.

Main Line Stations in Paris
Destinations
Gare St. Lazare: Suburbs, northern Normandy, Cherbourg, Dieppe, Le Havre
Gare du Nord: Lille, Calais, Boulogne, Belgium, Holland
Gare de l'Est: Strasbourg, Belfort, Germany
Gare de Lyon: TGV to Lyon, Marseille and the Côte d'Azur, Switzerland
Gare d'Austerlitz: South West: Toulouse, Perpignan, Bordeaux, Spain
Gare de Montparnasse: Brittany: Brest, Rennes, Le Mans

Airports
Charles de Gaulle: Intercontinental flights, and all Air France services
Orly: European and all charter flights. Air Inter

Coach stations
Porte de la Villette: Next to Métro; all international arrivals and departures. There are no long distance internal services from Paris, but some in the provinces, especially along the Mediterranean coast. These cost the same as the equivalent distance by train, and are much slower. However, they are good for sight-seeing, and call at some villages not served by the railway. They often connect with trains at the local stations.

Appendix C
British Consular Posts in Metropolitan France

Paris Consular District

1 British Embassy, Consular Section, 16 rue d'Anjou, 75383 PARIS Cedex 08. Tel: 42 66 91 42; Office hours (for public) 09.30–12.30, 14.30–17.00

2 British Consulate, 9 quai George V, 76600 LE HAVRE. Tel: 35 42 27 47; Office hours: 09.30–12.00 (Honorary Consul)

3 British Consulate, c/o Association France-Grande-Bretagne, 5 rue des Cadeniers, 40000 NANTES. Tel: 40 63 16 02; Office hours: 09.00–12.15, 14.00–17.00 (Honorary Consul)

4 British Consulate, Townsend Thoresen, Gare Maritime, 50101 CHERBOURG. Tel: 33 44 20 13; (Honorary Consul)

5 British Consulate, 'La Hulotte', 8 ave de la Libération, 35800 DINARD. Tel: 99 46 26 64; (Honorary Consul)

Bordeaux Consular District

1 British Consulate-General, 15 Cours de Verdun, 33081 BORDEAUX. Tel: 56 52 28 35; Open to Public: 09.00–12.00, 14.30–17.30

2 (Toulouse area), British Consulate, Lucas Aerospace, c/o Thomson CSF, BP 143, 15 ave Didier Daurat, 31702 BLAGNAC. Tel: 61 30 03 23 (Honorary Consul)

Lille Consular District

1 British Consulate-General, 11 square Dutilleul, 59800 LILLE. Tel: 20 57 87 90; Office Hours: 09.00–12.00, 14.00–17.30

2 British Consulate, c/o Electrodes Enrobées, 14 rue Gustave Courbet, 62107 CALAIS. Tel: 21 96 33 76 (Honorary Consul)

3 British Consulate, c/o British Railways, Gare Maritime, 62201 BOULOGNE-SUR-MER. Tel: 21 30 25 11; Office hours: 09.00–12.00, 14.00–17.00 (Honorary Consul)

4 British Consulate, c/o L. Deweulf, Cailleret & Fils, 11 rue des

Arbres, BP 1502, 59383 DUNKERQUE. Tel: 28 66 11 98; Office hours: Mondays and Fridays 08.30–12.00 (Honorary Consul)

Lyons Consular District
British Consulate-General, 24 rue Childebert, 69288 LYON Cedex 1. Tel: 78 37 59 67; Office hours: 09.30–12.30, 14.30 - 17.00

Marseilles Consular District
1 British Consulate-General, 24 ave du Prado, 13006 MAR-SEILLE. Tel: 91 53 43 32; 91 37 66 95; Office hours: 09.00–12.00, 14.00–18.00
2 British Consulate, 11 rue Paradis, 06000 NICE. Tel: 93 82 32 04; (Honorary Consul for Nice and Principality of Monaco).

Appendix D
English Language Bookstores Paris

Brentano, 31 Avenue de l'Opera, 75001.

FNAC (Fédération Nationale d'Anciens Combattants). Three large stores, at Les Halles, the rue de Renne and the Avenue Wagram, near the Etoile, all have a wide choice of books in English.

GALIGNANI, 226 de Rivoli.

Librairie Internationale, 82 Grande Rue, Sèvres 92310.

Marshall's Bookshop and Tearoom, 26 rue Brey, 75017 Paris 9 (near the Etoile).

W.H. Smith & Sons, 248 rue de Rivoli, near the Place de la Concorde.

Shakespeare & Co., 37 rue de la Bucherie, 75005.

The American Church, situated on the Quai d'Orsay, operates a 'Flea Market', or Bring and Buy sale, on most Saturday afternoons of the year, outside holiday periods, and English books are always on sale here. Some of the stalls on the banks of the Seine, the 'bouquinistes' have books in English, and these can also be found at the markets around the edges of Paris proper, at the Porte de Bagnolet, Porte de Clignancourt, and Porte des Lilas. However, other bargains have long been snapped up here.

Newspapers and magazines are sold from kiosks and shops throughout the city, and indeed throughout France. Those available in English almost everywhere include *The Times, The Daily Telegraph,* the *Financial Times,* the *Daily Mail,* the *Daily Express,* the *Daily Mirror,* of the British dailies; the *International Herald Tribune,* which is published in Paris every day, and carries American financial and sports information, as well as some general news and interesting articles. English language magazines include *The Economist, Time, Newsweek* and *Fortune;* depending on the clientele, others are available at selected kiosks.

Lending Libraries are operated by the British Council, rue Constantine, near the Invalides Métro; the Canadian Institute, next door to the British Council, and by the American Institute on the rue Valentin, 75007. French public libraries, situated in or near each *mairie* (Town Hall) often have quite a selection, although this tends to be limited to examination set texts, reference books, and the odd novel.

Index